NEW AND REVISED EDITION

Two Owls
at
Eton

A TRUE STORY

JONATHAN FRANKLIN

metro

Published by Metro Publishing,
an imprint of John Blake Publishing Limited,
3 Bramber Court, 2 Bramber Road,
London W14 9PB, England

www.johnblakebooks.com

www.facebook.com/johnblakebooks ▮
twitter.com/jblakebooks ▮

First published in 1960 by Putnam & Co. Ltd, London.
New and expanded edition first published in hardback in 2016

ISBN: 978-1-78606-030-3

British Library Cataloguing-in-Publication Data:
A catalogue record for this book is available from the British Library.

Design by www.envydesign.co.uk

Printed in Great Britain by CPI Group (UK) Ltd

1 3 5 7 9 10 8 6 4 2

Papers used by John Blake Publishing are natural, recyclable products
made from wood grown in sustainable forests. The manufacturing processes
conform to the environmental regulations of the country of origin.

Every attempt has been made to contact the relevant copyright-holders,
but some were unobtainable. We would be grateful if the appropriate people
could contact us.

This second edition is for
Annabel

Contents

Acknowledgements

The photographs in this book have been taken by the author and countless other amateur photographers, but those on pages, 105, 107, 109, 111, 114, 117 [plates pages 5 lower, 6 lower left, 8 lower] by Lieutenant-Colonel Manning, of Yoxford, Suffolk.

The drawings are by my fellow-Etonian and friend, Simon Radcliffe.

If I thanked all who I should it would take many pages, but I am extremely grateful to my House Master, Mr Hill, for all his support; also to Tim Curtis, a friend of mine, who helped me seek out many schoolboy mistakes. Finally, I cannot thank my father enough, without whose encouragement and final correcting I would not have written this story.

Acknowledgements for the second edition

In the first place, I must thank Toby Buchan of John Blake Publishing for proposing this second edition and seeing it through; also Jackie Tarrant-Barton of the Old Etonian Association for tracking me down.

I am also extremely grateful to my agent, Jemima Hunt of the Writers' Practice, for her wise counsel.

Introduction

When I was ten, I could tell you the wingspan and the colour of the eggs of every bird in *The Observer's Book of British Birds*. I would wander up and down Suffolk hedgerows collecting birds' eggs (today quite rightly that is illegal); only one from a nest was the rule. I would blow the yolk and white out and fry them up with fresh eel that I'd caught in a tidal pond beside the River Deben. Scrumptious.

I thought of myself as a budding ornithologist and leapt at the chance to look after a wounded bird or an abandoned fledgling. My first effort was to make a splint for the broken wing of a black-headed gull that I found in Kensington Gardens. I had to force feed it, but it died within three days. I knew I had to improve my technique.

By the time the heroes of this book, Dee and Dum, arrived at Eton, I had nursed a thrush, a jackdaw and a pigeon, and kept a baby rabbit, brought in by our cat, in my bed while I was recovering from flu.

But it was owls that fascinated and especially tawnies: the silent flight, the sharp, mysterious hooting, the soft brown plumage and the extraordinary swivel-like turning of the head. Examining a dead tawny, I was intrigued by the size of the eyes and the long semicircle of a hidden ear on each side of the flat round head. An ornithologist friend of mine told me that the eye socket of an owl takes up more than 60 per cent of its skull whereas ours takes up a mere 5 per cent, and that the design of a stealth bomber's wings owes much to detailed appreciation of owls' wings.

Dee and Dum, lucky to be alive, arrived at Eton in a simple cage and were adored by everyone who met them. I was sixteen. We grew up together in that summer of 1959.

*

I went to Eton because my father played cricket with my House Master and my mother knew several mothers of Etonians. In those days Eton was not the target of constant, global media attention but rather the object of mild curiosity; calling a term a Half, wearing formal School Dress in remembrance of George III and playing games like the Field and Wall games that no other school played. I arrived in my tails and white tie at just thirteen and, I admit, scared stiff. Discipline was rumoured to be fierce: Beating, Swiping, Tanning lay in the shadows ready to jump out. I felt utterly insignificant, surrounded by tall, elegant buildings, their walls hung with ancient pictures and tapestries. For the first few days I walked, head down, as if along an endless passage hemmed in by high walls where I couldn't see over the top and where to go.

At the time, the press was full of news of distant wars; the Suez Crisis and the Hungarian Uprising. We heard that an old boy from our house had been killed in the Malayan Emergency. My peer group of boys came from varied backgrounds, and there were some whose fathers had been killed in the Second World War. There were masters who had served – one had been a Lancaster bomber pilot, another a prisoner of the Japanese and because his neck was rather long we nicknamed him Rubber Neck as we imagined he had been stretched on a rack. We wondered whether we'd be called up when we left school. Some rather relished the prospect of banging about with a .303. Fortunately, Elvis was rocking out 'Hound Dog' and 'Blue Suede Shoes'.

I would walk up Eton High Street with a friend on the way to Agar's Plough to find a tree for Dee and Dum to clamber about in. No one thought it particularly strange that a boy should wander around school with a couple of owls on his shoulders. Duff Cooper once said that Eton allowed eccentricity and encouraged boys to follow their passions. How true.

I wrote this book at the suggestion of John Pudney of Putnam's. He had read my article about the owls in the school's Natural History Society magazine. He asked for a couple of chapters. He liked them and there I was writing a book. My House Master, Bud Hill, let me write by candlelight after Lights Out for two nights a week; amazing for a House Master who confiscated our longed-for Valentine cards, and equally surprising that both he and my parents let me spend so much time on such an ex-curriculum activity in my A-level year. My indifferent results were probably due to the attention my feathered babies demanded as they scuffled around my room and teased at my pen with their talons, resulting in even more incomprehensible French than usual.

INTRODUCTION

Apart from the absorbing interest in writing this book while still at school, I savoured my last year at Eton. School Library and College Library were magnets and I would admire the spines of rare books and occasionally dare to pull one out. In the evenings I would go to meetings of several of the school societies. There was a freedom to pursue your interest without influence or interference. Even so, every morning all Upper Boys had to assemble in that gem of European architecture, College Chapel, for the master in charge to make sure that no errant boy was larking about in London. The Precentor played Bach on the huge organ. Such is the strength of that organ that rumour has it that playing with all stops out helped to shake out the remaining shards of coloured glass from the stone window frames after a bomb had landed nearby during the war. I felt very *very* lucky.

*

This book was published in November 1960. Five extracts were serialised in the London *Evening Standard*. But still I was amazed to see a huge coloured billboard showing Dee and Dum in full flight on the paper's sales stand at the crossroads in the High Street.

I am sure that I walked past pink in the face and was probably mobbed up mercilessly by my friends. Within a fortnight we were in the *Evening Standard's* Top Ten bestseller list. The week before there had been extracts from a biography of Lord Curzon and one critic expressed his relief that memories of that 'Most superior person' had been fluffed away by a couple of birds! The next day a girl I'd always fancied wrote saying that she'd just walked past Liberty's in Regent Street and that a whole window was dedicated to my book, with at least three hundred copies on display. I hoped that my chances might improve with her. But no, Dee and Dum didn't win on that one.

I was to leave Eton for the last time that Christmas. Robert Birley, the Headmaster, asked me to lunch. He said that Dee and Dum had done more good for the school's image than any other recent publication. That, certainly, was worth a bonus mouse for Dee.

And then BBC *Look East* rang wanting a live interview. I drifted about in a haze of incredulity with no idea of the fame that was about to hit Dee and Dum. Even Walt Disney played with the idea of an animated cartoon. Often a well-meaning hostess at her daughter's coming-out party would insist that I sat beside her to talk about owls; whereas all I wanted to do was to be next to her daughter as a prelude to the last dance of the evening, hopefully cheek to cheek.

Often as I walked to work down the King's Road in London, there would be a pat on my shoulder and a friendly greeting of, 'Hello, Owls. How's life?'

And then I left for France and on to Brazil. But owls didn't forget us. Often, at my mother's house in Suffolk, a cardboard box with no message, just a plain box, would be on front doorstep and we'd know what was inside: one, two and even, once, three baby owls. We'd become a safe haven for distressed owls. Over fifteen years we nursed and released between eighteen and twenty abandoned tawny and barn owls.

Even in Brazil, owls refused to forget me. I was given two immature least pygmy owls. Tiny little chestnut, yellow-eyed, fierce predators, no bigger than my fist, that live in burrows. An armadillo had probably wrecked their nest. I spent hours with them but failed to make friends, and eventually and very sadly they died of bad chicken heads from the local butcher because I'd run out of fresh sparrows. I was devastated at my failure.

*

Today, I understand that, due to the fame of Hedwig, the owl in the Harry Potter books, perfectly healthy owlets are taken from their nests to be somebody's Hedwig. I expect many die within days. I implore that this book does not encourage any such robbery. Owls are wild animals and we must do our best to protect them, especially in these times of intense agricultural practices. To look after an owlet is a full-time job. You can't leave one in a room and expect it to be happy. If you want to help, put up owl boxes. They are effective. Every owl that my mother and I brought up was an orphan or damaged, and our object was to get them back into the wild as soon as possible.

On a balmy autumn evening, with a glass of wine to hand, I sit in the garden a few yards away from where Dee and Dum began to gain enough confidence to return to the wild. I listen with pleasure to the shrill hooting and sharp squawks as the descendants of Dee and Dum (as much Old Etonians as George Orwell and Prince William) squabble with their children and shoo them out, as parents are wont to do.

SEPTEMBER 2016

CHAPTER I

Arrival

From yonder ivy-mantled tow'r
The moping owl does to the moon complain.

Thomas Gray 'Elegy Written in a
Country Churchyard'

THE PORCH OF Debenhams in London's Oxford
Street was filled with a crowd of people; all eyes
were fixed on one object. Little did I know that the
centre of their attention was my pair of owls in their
cage. There they were, squatting on their haunches,
quietly contemplating the chattering mass of onlookers.
I pushed my way through, excited at the thought of
seeing them for the first time for two weeks.

It all started one day late in April when a friend
rang me up to tell me he had a nest of tawny owls in
his garden; would I like one? Apparently the mother
had been shot by a gamekeeper and there were some

young orphans left. It annoyed me very much to hear this, as the constant massacre of owls is pointless; they do incomparably more good than harm. On the other hand I was excited to hear about the babies, because owls have always fascinated me. Not thinking of the complications involved, I immediately said 'yes'. This one word changed the whole routine of my life for a good year.

The nest was in a hollow tree and held two babies. I immediately broached the subject of having them with my parents, who were decidedly against the idea. Who, they asked, would look after them when I went back to school in a week and they had to leave for the Continent? I suggested Susan, our gardener's daughter. There was no reply to this idea except a quiet 'Poor thing' from my sister. However, I knew the answer was 'no'.

The subject arose again at breakfast with my father, as I thought that if I could persuade him, my animal-loving mother would soon agree. The argument waxed hot and tempers rose. I kept saying that we could not let them die and must save them and bring them up. Then, I had the brainwave of taking the owls back to school with me. They were very small and could not possibly cause any trouble. This complicated the issue rather than simplified it and remarks such as 'Never heard of such a thing, *owls* at Eton!' were frequent. My father is not at his best at the breakfast table. However, a temporary arrangement was reached. I must write to M'Tutor (that is, my House Master) and ask him if I could bring them back to school. If he said yes, wonderful, if no, I hoped Susan would take on the job of nursemaid for me, as she is very fond of animals.

I did not write the letter until two days before school began, only just leaving time for a reply to arrive on the morning before I left home. Meanwhile I collected the owls from their tree fifteen miles away, helped by a very kind friend, Mrs Hawdon. We both went armed with leather gloves and scarves to protect our eyes, as I had read that owls in the mating season are more courageous than any hawk.

I found the hole was just within ladder height and climbed up. Peering in, I could see two small balls of fluffy white down. They seemed to consist only of stomachs and mouths and into these, although the owls were only the size of tennis balls, I could insert my thumb. They were lying in a makeshift nest of old pellets and bones, surrounded by dead rats and mice.

When owls catch their prey – rats, mice, voles,

moles, baby rabbits and the occasional fish taken on the surface – they do not necessarily eat it immediately but put it beside their nests. This is a useful habit, as in winter food can be scarce for days on end and so the hungry owl can then resort to this reserve. These stored animals are often decomposed but an owl will eat almost any rotting food.

As I looked at them, I felt very doubtful whether I could hope to rear babies so young; they were only three weeks old. But when the larger, sensing my presence, turned towards me and gave a loud click with its beak I could not resist the temptation to pick them up and put them into a cloth-lined box.

The journey home was uneventful and the owls lay quietly in their box. They were the ugliest baby creatures I had ever seen and at first I felt disappointed. Their heads were one and a half inches in diameter, with two red slits where the eyes were eventually to appear, and an enormous opening which was the beak. The head and body, connected by a thin neck, were covered with a sparse layer of white fluff. They had only tiny stubs of flesh for wings and little white immature legs. Unable to walk, they were completely helpless. They were only capable of opening their mouths, clicking their beaks and making raucous cries, which they did whenever I lifted the lid. I am convinced it was not for fright and more likely for food as they were still blind.

The first problem when I arrived home was food. I had read *The Observer's Book of Birds,* and other books, and all said that owls eat rats, mice, etc. But I had been told that baby owls are given the insides of animals until they are old enough to eat fur and feathers, which are roughage for them. That night I fed them with plain horsemeat and halibut oil and put them in the airing cupboard in the kitchen, which I thought would keep them sufficiently warm. As I put them into the cupboard our housekeeper turned to me and said, 'Won't they cook?' For a moment I was horror-struck as the thought of cooked owl for breakfast flashed through my mind, but I soon remembered the many other small birds who had started their recovery in our airing cupboard. I went to bed that night thinking what horrible, ugly little beasts my future pets were.

At six o'clock next morning they were ravenous. Beside the larger of the two lay a small round ball of fur and feathers, the technical name of which is a 'pellet'. A pellet consists of undigested particles of food, bones, feathers and fur, which are separated from the flesh by an iron-hard stomach that nature has placed below the breast-bone, not above as in the case of the crops of other birds. These pellets are regurgitated at twelve-hour intervals and vary in size according to the amount the bird has eaten. My owls produced quite small ones, from one and a half inches long and a third to half an inch thick, because they had more boneless food than wild owls. The pellets of wild owls can be over two inches long and half an inch wide. I once found one with three mouse skulls in it.

I had heard of one or two cases where people keeping owls had lost them due to what I thought was a bad diet and in particular not enough roughage to produce pellets. My biology teacher said that these pellets are of vital importance to an owl, because in its stomach there would be a strong secretion or enzyme that helps to break up the bodies of their prey, and unless this secretion is disposed of through a regular pellet and not left unused in its stomach, it could paralyse and eventually kill. In the wild this presents no problem, as owls only eat furred and feathered creatures. I was terrified lest anything like this should happen to mine, so I immediately started covering the meat with feathers and fur. I also set five mouse traps, and caught six mice, two in one, side by side!

While I was preparing the food, I noticed that the bigger of the two was pecking at his brother, who was now quite still. Very soon I realised that this pecking was no affectionate caress, but plain cannibalism! The other owl woke up and proceeded to try to eat his brother also. The only explanation possible is that in their blind state they mistook each other for food. This habit lasted until well after their eyes had opened; it must therefore have been due to a lack of brotherly love! Meanwhile the day for returning to school was approaching and the time for an answer from my House Master. In case of a refusal I prepared everything for Susan; pages of instructions, clean bedding, mouse-skins (as we gave only the skins at this stage), horsemeat, liver as their main food, tins of chicken pellets, and a bottle of precious halibut oil which I felt was life-giving to them.

I started feeding them chicken pellets when I saw a sack being taken to the chicken-house. On it was written 'Extra Vitamins' and so after that I gave them some Spillers Chick Crumbs. I hoped these would fight off any possible paralysis that I'd been warned about, due to lack of vitamins. I soaked the crumbs in water and made them into soft lumps. They smelt revolting, but the owls ate them up readily enough.

The fateful morning arrived and with it no return letter. I had not given my House Master enough time to answer. And so with a heavy heart, as I had already become fond of my ugly companions, I left them in Susan's hands. The letter arrived by the afternoon post just after I had left home and when I arrived at Eton M'Tutor immediately asked me where the owls were and if they were all right!

For the next fortnight I did not see them but was assured that they were in good health by frequent letters from Susan. In my anxiety I wrote frantic letters asking for news and giving instructions which were either impossible to carry out or quite useless. I wrote continually to find out if they had made a pellet, as I was frightened lest they should die. Each letter said, 'Put more feathers on the meat, put more fur on, for heaven's sake. Please watch day and night to see if they produce one.' Each reply letter was the same, 'Sorry, I am afraid there is no pellet yet.' By the end of ten days I had sent five letters and was indeed in a state of desperation, knowing that the next letter would bring news of a pellet or of death.

One morning there was as usual a letter lying on my breakfast plate. The address stood out clearly, 'J. M. Franklin, Esq., Corner House.' I picked it up with trembling hands and tore it open. There was one line, 'I found a pellet this morning'!

Susan kept the owls in a cloth-lined box in an airing cupboard and fed them at regular intervals, in spite of her having to go to school. Feeding times were: 7.30, a large breakfast; 10.30, a light meal, given by Susan's mother; 12.30, a large lunch, given by Susan; 3.30, a light meal; 7, another meal and 10.30, a large supper to last them through the night.

The food was mainly horsemeat covered with pigeon feathers or fur, pieces of mice and a little liver, plus one drop of halibut oil each per day. They were given as much as they could eat and as a result grew tremendously. In two weeks they were twice their former size. Their appetites were enormous and in a week they consumed half a pound of horsemeat and a quarter of a pound of liver, to say nothing of the many mice which were trapped every day.

When the owls were fed, the food was prepared first and put on a plate. They were seated on the table on their behinds with their feet out in front and heads up like begging dogs. At first they rolled over but soon their legs strengthened and helped them to keep upright. Also, their stomachs were so big and protruded so far that they hardly needed other help.

The food was put down their open mouths in small bits. Water was squirted down once a day from an eye-dropper.

Very shortly they outgrew their box and began to wake Susan up in the morning with their beak clickings and raucous cries and so they were transferred into an old budgerigar cage. Susan put this in the kitchen and they spent the day either sleeping or watching with intense curiosity every movement made outside their cage. They would sit motionless and follow the object of interest through its entire course by turning only their heads and watching with unblinking eyes like two old women. Owls cannot move their eyes, only their heads.

Their limbs soon began to strengthen and they began to walk and climb. When climbing they clambered up the side of the cage. This exercise would take anything up to a quarter of an hour. When it reached the top, the owl, unable to think of a means of descent, would loose its grip and fall to the ground with a sickening thud, where it would lie struggling on its back. Shrieks of laughter would come from Susan and her sister Doreen, whereupon the owl would give a convulsive jerk and right itself and then gaze at the source of noise until the laughter ceased. When it did, the climbing would start again. It would go on until both owls were so exhausted that they fell asleep.

After two weeks of the half, i.e. term, I broached the subject of having the owls at Eton to my House Master again. Fortunately he did not object, and very soon I had a plan to bring them to school.

I managed to arrange a dentist appointment in London, when my friend, Mrs Hawdon, would be going there as well. She agreed to bring the owls with her and we fixed the meeting place to be in the hall of Debenhams, as it was near my dentist.

Mrs Hawdon fetched the owls from Susan, put them in a large mouse-cage, 2 foot 6 inches by 1 foot 6 inches by 1 foot 6 inches, and caught the train to London after a restless night, as the owls had decided to spend it pecking the wire of the cage. On the train she sat proudly beside her charges and fended off all questions. However, halfway to London she had to leave the carriage to have her breakfast. Returning, she found a crowd of people in the corridor with one man gesticulating wildly and nursing a finger. With his other hand he was pointing menacingly in the direction of the cage. My friend pushed her way into the compartment, fearing to find the owls carried off as a danger to the public but she found them fast asleep.

After much shouting and indignant protest from the wounded man, the story unfolded itself. This man, fancying his influence over animals, had approached the cage, and with cooing noises had tried to stroke one of the owls. The owl, however, feeling hungry, mistook the finger for a worm and, grabbing it in his beak for all his worth, refused to let go until the man pulled it out by force. Eventually tempers calmed and, nursing his injured finger, the man left the train, vowing never to try to make friends with owls again.

On arrival at Debenhams, the cage was placed in the porch and Mrs Hawdon sat patiently beside it until I should arrive. I arrived five minutes later, to find a large crowd already assembled. I forced my way through the crowd and, without paying any attention to my friend, such was my hurry, knelt down beside the cage and gazed at its contents. The owls were twice the size they had been when I had left them two weeks before and were now alert and attractive to look at. They had grown new downy feathers which were light grey in colour with stripes of dark grey and brown.

The next stage of the journey entailed getting them to Waterloo Station from where I could catch a train to Eton. I hailed a taxi, while Mrs Hawdon and the commissionaire brought out the cage and the boxes of food. As the taxi drew up I said to the driver in a merry voice, 'You don't know what you're taking on, old chap.' He looked at me faintly bored and then stiffened as he saw the commissionaire advancing with the cage. 'That isn't coming in here, is it?' he asked, scowling at me. 'Oh, yes, it is,' I replied as I bundled myself and the cage into the taxi, at the same time thanking and saying goodbye to Mrs Hawdon. Then turning to the driver I told him where to go. Before I had finished, the taxi was bounding forward down Oxford Street with the driver bent over the wheel and his accelerator hard down.

It was the fastest taxi drive I have ever experienced. Every now and then the driver would look over his shoulder, possibly expecting me to turn into an owl at any moment. As I paid him off at Waterloo, I thought I saw drops of sweat on his brow but perhaps it was only my imagination!

I picked up the cage and held it at arm's length so that I could just see over the top and walked up the steps towards the suburban lines. At the top I marched firmly forward, but hardly had I gone five paces when I saw something which made me stop dead in my tracks. Walking towards me, ten yards away, were the two most august dignitaries of Eton: Provost Elliot and

Vice-Provost Lambard. My blood froze and I remained rooted to the spot. Perhaps they would recognise me and put a stop to my plans then and there. I looked around for a place to hide. Behind me I saw a flight of dirty steps, down which I scurried like an overloaded burglar escaping from the police. I found myself in one of those palatial marble halls of the Victorian era, usually described as Gentlemen's Cloakrooms. In spite of the surroundings I put the owls on the floor and stood gasping for breath.

Five minutes later I emerged, rather cautiously, to find that the dignitaries were no longer in sight. I walked up to the timetable, put the owls on the ground again and started to look for my train. As I was doing so I heard various comments from behind, 'Oh, aren't they sweet!' 'The little darlings!' 'Oh, the poor things!' 'Are they chinchillas?' Somewhat embarrassed, I walked past a sleepy-looking ticket-clipper so fast that he could not see what I was carrying, climbed into the nearest carriage and sank into a corner, thankful to be away from the public gaze at last. Fortunately there were only two other people in the carriage, one in the middle of each side.

My peace of mind was short-lived.

I noticed that both the other occupants seemed to

be getting further away from me. Sure enough, there they were, slowly edging away until they had reached the furthest possible distance from my owls. There, in truly British fashion, they pulled out their evening papers and became immersed in them. I felt hot under the collar; surely they did not think I was mad?

This train was a rush-hour train, but nobody else came into our carriage. Occasionally, somebody would stop and look in, but they always passed on. When the whistle went, however, about six people rushed in all at once. I ignored them and looked at my owls properly for the first time.

Their eyes, now open, were big and a bluey dark brown, but there was still a red rim around the eyelids. The eyelids and eye cavities were covered with minute, very thin feathers. Their heads and bodies had thick grey-brown downy feathers becoming darker towards the roots with dark brown streaks, making a highly complicated pattern. The wings and tails were almost non-existent; the tail being smothered with downy feathers only half an inch long. The wings were feathery arms with a few primaries just peeping through on the last point. Their legs were beginning to put on the characteristic trouser feathers and had grown considerably, but still did not have enough strength to support the whole weight of their bodies for any length of time.

At first they lay placidly on their stomachs in the cage, but after a short time they began to show some signs of movement. Every so often one of them would rise manfully to its feet and walk slowly across the cage. This it did in a horizontal position with its eyes looking at the ground and legs working frantically behind. The inevitable was bound to happen. After three or four paces the owl would fall flat on its face, legs poking out behind. A violent struggle would ensue, in which legs and wings were thrown in all directions until it realised all was hopeless, whereupon it would close its eyes and try to sleep. Then, either from curiosity about its surroundings or enthusiasm to learn the art of walking, in a few minutes the eyes would open again and the head would rise, turn completely around through 180 degrees, and look at every object in turn. This manoeuvre was carried out with the rest of the body still flat on the ground and quite motionless. After this, the owl would decide to struggle on to his behind again, and the whole proceedings would begin all over again.

After a quarter of an hour I noticed that all the passengers had stopped reading; all eyes were riveted on the two fluffy objects, which now looked like proper owls and were very pretty. For the rest of the journey there were eight owl-worshippers, including myself, loving these charming and comical creatures.

My arrival back at my house was heralded with cheers and shouts of, 'Hello, Owlman,' and suchlike. Everybody rushed up to my room and began to maul my poor birds in such a manner that I was surprised they survived. They had gone down well with my friends, but my main anxiety was the opinion of my House Master, Mr Hill.

He heard about them on his goodnight rounds. 'Oh, sir, have you seen Franklin's owls?'

'What?' came the reply. 'He hasn't got those things, has he?' and immediately he strode up the stairs to my room.

I heard his steps coming down the passage and prepared for the worst. My door burst open.

'Where are your owls?' he asked quickly. I pointed gingerly at the innocent and unsuspecting owls.

'Oh! Aren't they sweet!' he exclaimed and kneeling down he began to scrutinise them. After a short time he stood up.

'May I get my wife and daughter to come and see them?'

'Of course, sir.'

A quarter of an hour later I was left assured that there would be no complaints from M'Tutor and his wife; their hearts were won. I have had only encouragement and great interest from M'Tutor, although there have been some troublesome moments.

That night I fed them on the food provided by Susan: hare's ear, horsemeat and pigeon feathers and halibut oil. I put them to bed on a cardboard sheet in their cage with no cover over the top. I went to bed confident that the owls and I would sleep the sleep of the exhausted.

But the owls had different plans for that night and their newfound master. After an hour or so, at about eleven o'clock, they began to pace up and down, scratching the cardboard with their claws and creating a nerve-racking noise. Not content with this, one decided to peck the wire. Finding it gave out a pleasant noise, he immediately gave it violent tweaks. The other soon began merrily to accompany his brother. The noise was ear-shattering and sounded like an enormous out-of-tune double bass. I jumped out of bed and made the owls lie down. This had no effect. As soon as I was in bed the noises started up again, both twanging and scraping. I screamed some unprintable word and there was silence, this time for about fifteen minutes, at the end of which the awful twanging started again. For the next hour I shouted abuse at them at regular intervals and came to the conclusion that my owls were musical.

When finally sleep came, I was so content to have my owls at last with me that I gave no thought to the difficulties and also the great hilarities that would arise in my efforts to keep them alive over the following few weeks.

CHAPTER II

Schooldays

Of all clean birds ye shall eat. But these are they of
which ye shall not eat: . . . and the owl and the night hawk,
and the cuckoo . . . the little owl and the great owl.

DEUTERONOMY 14: 11–16

I SHALL NEVER FORGET the next day. The owls woke
me at 5.30 a.m. with squawks and twangs,
complaining that they were hungry. The only food I
had was some rather bad horsemeat Susan had sent
and some feathers that looked as if they had come out
of a pillow. They ate this unappetising breakfast with
relish and cleared up the whole plate of the little balls
of fur and meat. I was soon out of provisions.

When their stomachs were bursting I put them side
by side on some paper in a corner between the cage
and my wash-box. Immediately their eyes drooped

and they fell fast asleep without any protest. I went back to bed and fell asleep myself.

At 6.45 I was woken, as usual, by the 'Boys' Maid' and had to get ready for 'Early School' at 7.30. My two companions were still asleep, flat on their stomachs. Treading softly, I washed and dressed, collected my books, and then peeped over the top of the wash-box to see if they were still asleep. As I did so, the larger of the two lifted up its head and squawked. Immediately the other woke up and both started to squawk as loud as they could. They were hungry and I had nothing to give them. There were five minutes to the beginning of school and half a mile to go!

I looked at them, sitting there, squawking plaintively and pleading with their eyes. I leant down and they immediately seized my finger. Panic struck me. How could I leave them alone?

I picked them up, turned them over on to their stomachs and started to stroke them, saying softly, 'Sleep, sleep.' At last their heads dropped and the squawks became fainter and fainter until their eyes closed and they were asleep.

Two minutes left until school started. I ran the whole way only to find the Beak already there.

'Why are you late?' he growled.

'Sorry, sir, I've been putting my owls to sleep,' I gasped, not thinking how ridiculous that must have sounded.

The Beak glared at me, blinked owlishly himself, took off his glasses and, after carefully wiping them, replaced them on his nose.

'Sit down,' he said in a bored tone.

I rushed back from Early School, ate my breakfast in five minutes and ran upstairs. I looked nervously over the top of the wash-box. They were gone! Nothing – except a few grey-brown feathers – was left where I had put them.

Wildly I searched the room. I found one asleep under the bed and the other, also asleep, under the table. Their walking had obviously improved since the journey of the day before. This was the first of many frights I had when finding no owls in my room.

After breakfast soon became routine. There was just three-quarters of an hour between the time I finished my breakfast and Chapel.

As soon as I had made my bed I put it up, which meant folding it in half and tying the two ends with a strap. A board with material hanging down the sides goes on top, thus making an extra, higher, table. On this the owls would spend their day. Before breakfast the smaller of the two found that the floor was the more comfortable place, especially when wedged in between the cage and the wash-box. The bigger, being slightly older, preferred to get on the top of the cage by scrambling up the side. He would then stand on one leg. In this position, with the other owl directly underneath, he would try to go to sleep. Often he succeeded. I always knew when he had, because there would be a slight thud, followed by a chorus of sharp cries and squawks as the two tried to disentangle themselves one from the other.

On top of the folded-up bed they were quite happy practising their walking or falling asleep. They both realised that a good lying position was at right angles to the edge with just their heads hanging over. Like this, they could peer down at the floor and by moving their heads from side to side they could see into every other part of the room as well. It is said that someone is as 'wise as an owl' but I would add 'curious' as well.

Other jobs to do before Chapel were to wash their bed and go to the butcher to buy their food. After the first night, I changed their bed to a cloth-covered piece of cardboard which deadened the scratching sound of their talons. Naturally food was an all-important matter. The butcher, however, was right at the other end of Eton, about half a mile away and walking there was the job I hated most. I got to know the policeman on that beat, and he soon found out the reason for my daily walk. He would place himself where I was bound to pass, always greeting me with some singularly original remark such as, 'Hungry birds, owls!' as, hot and tired, I carried that day's rations back to my house.

I covered the room with paper. Every visible spot always had at least two or three sheets on it so removing a mess was easy. Just before Chapel I fed them again. The next large meal was at lunchtime, when they were always ravenous, and a further one at teatime. At 6 p.m. I would go out and dig for worms or, later on when they could fly, take them out for exercise. Between 9.30 and 10.15 p.m. I gave them their last meal and put them to bed.

Putting them to bed was quite the most exhausting task of the day, since as soon as the lights went out at 9.45 I had to rely on my torch. The owls knew very well that this was not adequate and there would be a mad chase around the room. They either ran on their flat feet or, once they could, flew. They found very original hiding places like under the grate of my fireplace or in my cricket boots. When caught, there would be a volley of piercing squawks and they would scratch until blood and bad language flowed quite freely. Sometimes if they were really lively I would put on a fives glove, make them sit on my protected hand and move my arm vigorously up and down. This caused them to lose their balance and flap their wings. In the end I would put two physically worn-out owls to sleep in their cage. I always placed a saucer within their reach with a little food just in case they felt hungry. I need hardly say that it was often empty in the morning.

Once they were in the cage, I covered them over with my dressing-gown to put them in complete darkness and to keep them quiet. One night, I was again woken up by that ear-shattering twanging. No amount of abuse from my bed stopped it, so I jumped out in a raging temper. I wrenched them out of their cage and started to flick at them with my forefinger as I thought their mother might do with her beak – not very hard, naturally. I hissed noisily at the same time. When my temper had cooled and I thought that they had had sufficient punishment, I replaced them in the cage and got back into bed. There wasn't another squeak.

In the morning there was peace in the room, unlike the normal rumpus that started the day. Had I hurt them, or even killed them? I rushed over to the cage and tore off the dressing-gown. At the other end of the cage, there they were huddled up together. They peered anxiously at me, wondering if they were in for it again. Feeling very ashamed, I picked them out and stroked them, trying to show that all was forgiven. They soon cheered up and began calling for breakfast. But never again did they wake me up during the night.

When they had been at school for a week and were obviously not going to die, the problem of what I was going to call them arose. My classical education made me think of the gods and goddesses of wisdom from Greek mythology, as owls are traditionally regarded as wise. But the names Minerva and Apollo sounded so ridiculous that I soon dropped that idea. I then thought of ordinary names like Jack and Jill and Bill and Mary – I was convinced that one was a girl and one a boy – but these names did not appeal either.

Then I happened to see a copy of *Through the Looking-Glass* and saw a picture of those memorable characters Tweedledum and Tweedledee. I thought how similar they were to my owls with their plump, round bodies. I named them after those two and soon after they were known to their friends as Dum and Dee.

Perhaps it seems curious that they were different in size. This is quite normal with owls because the mother lays a first egg and sits on it for a few days. Then she lays another, and so on, until she has laid about three in all. By the time she has laid the last, the first has hatched and the newborn babe is able to keep the other eggs warm. At this stage the mother may lay yet another, which will also be kept warm by the rest of the family. This is not easy for the newly hatched as it means the two eldest are, of course, very much stronger than the others. The last-hatched baby seldom survives and more often than not is decapitated or eaten by his brothers and sisters, especially if bad weather prevents the parents catching enough food. In the case of my two, Dum was obviously the elder and I referred to her as 'she', and Dee, the younger and smaller, as 'he'. With owls, the larger of the two sexes is usually the female.

They were always very excited in the early morning

when I let them out of the cage, especially when they had learnt to flutter a few yards. At 6.30 they would wake me up by jumping up and banging their heads against the top of the cage. Another way was to peck the empty saucer, but never did they twang the wire again!  When I let them out they would both, in their eagerness, jump for the hole in the top of the cage. The cage was opened at the top by a small door. This hole was too small for  both to fit through together and they invariably got stuck. Their bodies were thus firmly wedged side by side and they could only kick with their legs and frantically move their heads about. At last, after a  struggle, they would emerge and stand victorious on top of the cage.

By this time I would be back in bed.

At first Dum and Dee would stand completely still, looking at me in bed. Then quite suddenly they would start to move their heads in a

circular fashion, apparently through 360 degrees, as if double-jointed. They kept their bodies quite rigid but every few seconds would stand on different legs. This created a queer swaying motion, from which no doubt the expression 'as drunk as an owl' has come. I watched, fascinated.

After two or three minutes they would decide that nothing had changed in the room since the day before. Dee would crouch down and spring and half-flutter to my ottoman, two yards away. Once there, he would again survey the room with his drunken motion, but after half a minute or so, he would spring up and flutter and land in the fireplace, where I had prepared a soft bed for him. Landing, he would turn fiercely around and glare out of his retreat like a dog guarding its kennel. A few moments later he would lie down facing into the room and every now and then revolve his head in a few circles if anything attracted his attention.

Dum would come in the other direction, towards my bed. She'd spring and flutter on to the wash-box, a yard distant. Sometimes she would reach the top, other times fall short on to my towel, which hung over a rail. Immediately the towel would begin to slip and Dum would scramble upwards to keep her balance, rather like a dog in a treadmill working a spit. The calamity came when the towel ended and then with a squawk and a bump, towel and Dum would land in a heap on the floor.

Then all over again: spring to cage, to wash-box and to the table six inches from the wash-box. Once on the table she would begin to advance slowly with a cautious swaying walk. Every few steps she would stop and scrutinise some object, moving her head from side to side. At the end of the table there was a three-yard gap to my bed. To accomplish this great flight Dum had to concentrate and balance herself. She would crouch very low with her wings half-spread, and then jump and flap to the edge of my bed. She would now take great pleasure in walking on tip-toe very slowly and carefully over the whole length of my left leg and body. It tickled abominably, but I forced myself to bear it, not wishing to disturb her. Once on my shoulders she would inspect my face, gently nibble my ears and nose and tweak at my hair. When bored, she would leap on to my boot-box-cum-bedside-table, stand on one leg and solemnly survey the room with pompous interest.

One morning when I was feeling rather sleepy, I let the owls out and went back to sleep with my arm forming a triangle with my head. When I woke up I felt a soft fluffy object next to my right cheek. I opened my eye and there, half an inch from my eye, was Dum's beak. Seeing I was awake, she opened her eyes and began to peck the bridge of my nose. When one's nose is pecked by a beak designed to tear a rat to pieces it hurts, so I shook my head. This made Dum bite even tighter. In desperation, I blew strongly through my mouth upwards into Dum's belly against the growth line of her feathers. With a frightened squawk she released her hold and jumped out of my arms. Not wanting to discourage her friendliness I tried to persuade her that my nose was not to be used as a plaything, especially in the early morning, but she didn't understand and my nose always remained a target.

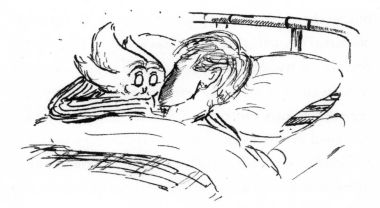

At this stage they were about six or seven weeks old and the fluffy grey down was beginning to come off. This did not mean that whole grey feathers came out, but the fluff grew out of the ends of the next growth and was shaken off, the majority rubbing off during the night against the wire of the cage. The next growth was grey-brown intermingled with other feathers of a deep russet-brown which was to be the final plumage. These were more prominent on the head, the middle of the back and the wings and tail, where the primaries and secondaries were in full growth. The feathers were not completely brown but had very dark brown streaks at an angle to each other, pointing to the centre of the feather. This created a fish-bone formation and gave the owls an appearance that ornithologists describe as 'mottled brown'. Their legs had almost completely put on their characteristic trousers and their claws had hardened to such an extent that I had to wear gloves to protect my hands. Their eyes still had red rims, which were beginning to sprout minute feathers, while the eye sockets had put on a light rufous colour which darkened by the week. Their mouths were enormous and could quite easily swallow the pieces of food I gave them, which were about half an inch in diameter.

At this stage also, they began to grow moustaches,

consisting of very thin dark feathers. These grew at the edge of the mouth and can be clearly seen in the photographs, giving them an appearance of critical old women.

Feeding was the major problem and caused me constant worry, since I had been told how easy it was for them to get rickets. While they had been at home they had been fed on horsemeat, liver, chick crumbs, halibut oil, feathers, mice, sparrows and rats caught in the garden. At school I could only get meat, liver, chick crumbs and halibut oil, or at least so I thought. I easily bought the meat and liver, and the chick crumbs came from home. Once a parcel came, which contained four sparrows that Susan had painstakingly caught. By the time they arrived, however, they were quite liquid, and did they smell!

Just when I thought that I had their diets running smoothly, with the usual meat and daily halibut oil, they both decided to go off their feed and would not touch any of the food I had so carefully prepared. I spent much time sitting in front of them with a piece of meat held invitingly in my fingers and with an anxious expression on my face. They hardly ate anything for two days and I thought they might be ill. I offered them the best beefsteak I could buy but they just turned up their noses at it. Lamb I never tried as I had been told it was bad for them. The only thing they did accept was liver, but I was very loath to give them only this as I had been warned against this as well.

Matters soon became desperate and they seemed to grow smaller before my eyes, so I began giving them more liver and feathers. Their eyes lit up when they ate it and they flapped their wings and clicked their beaks in eagerness to have more. As a result, their main food became liver plus the occasional other tempting morsel and on this diet they have always flourished, in spite of the books I have read and the contrary advice I have received.

When I fed them I used to whistle, hoping that eventually, when back in the wild, they would fly to me at my whistle. My whistle was short and on the same note. Very soon they began to take notice of it and after two weeks or so, they would genuinely get excited and stop doing whatever they were doing and look at me with eager eyes.

I soon found that their eyes were the most expressive that I have ever looked into. They were a dark bluey-brown without any white. The pupil part in the middle was dark blue while the surrounding iris was flecked with brown. They were lovely and coupled beautifully with their vocal language, vividly portraying hunger, eagerness, excitement, anger and happiness.

Their vocal language was varied and frequent; some I am sure, if translated, was not too pleasant. When hungry they would just squawk in rather a loud and raucous tone. If merely conversational, their squawk dropped to a murmur. This would continue for great lengths of time when they lay on my shoulder or sat on my lap. They showed acute anger with a volley of *Tch, tch* in a very high tone, and nervousness and fear by clicking their beaks together, a noise which can be produced by putting the tongue on the roof of your mouth and pulling down. And so with their expressive eyes and varied language, Dee, Dum and I soon came to understand each other.

CHAPTER III

Educating
the Wise

They say the owl was a baker's daughter.
WILLIAM SHAKESPEARE, *HAMLET*

B Y THE TIME they had been at Eton for two weeks and were seven weeks old, the news that I had owls had spread around in all circles of school society and little parcels of food began to arrive. One morning there was a large oblong packet waiting for me as I came back from Early School and was about to go into breakfast. I took it upstairs, curious to see what it was, as boys do not send messages to each other until after breakfast. I unwrapped the strange object quickly and was immediately repelled at the sight that met my eyes. There, lying on the table, was the largest rat I had ever seen. Needless to say I ate very little breakfast! Apparently a kind master's cat had caught this vast rodent in the early hours of the morning and presented it to him when he woke up. The master had immediately sent it to me, knowing of no better use for it. His cat proved very useful in days to come.

After breakfast I ran upstairs, eager to see what the owls would think of natural food. The rat was enormous, with great yellow fangs and powerful feet. I tied it by its tail to a piece of string and looked for an owl to tempt with this dainty morsel.

Dum was sitting on the ottoman, which was underneath my window and had the curtains hanging over two corners at the back. Dee was walking about the floor investigating everything in his usual inquisitive manner. I decided to try the experiment on Dum. And so with the rat on the end of the string, held at arm's length, I advanced towards her.

She was standing on one leg with her eyes half-closed, nearly asleep. Suddenly her eyes opened wide and became even rounder than usual. First a look of absolute horror passed over her face and then fear flashed into her eyes. She was afraid of a *rat*! Immediately her beak clicked violently and her wings sprang up, making her look twice her normal size. She started to back away from the approaching yellow-fanged monster. The edge of the ottoman soon stopped her retreat and she was cornered. Suddenly, however, the display of wings dropped and with a squeak Dum fled into the shelter of one of the hanging curtains. For a few seconds there was no movement, and then, very slowly, a small round head with two frightened eyes peered around the edge of the curtain. 'Dum,' I pleaded, 'this is your breakfast!' Dum blinked and kept her eyes riveted on the rat.

'Coward!' I thought, and turned around to look for Dee. He was still walking around the unfolded bed.

'Dee,' I called. 'Breakfast!'

Dee turned around quickly, expecting a tasty morsel of liver and pigeon feathers. Instead, six inches from his face hung my rat. Immediately his eyes showed fear and his wings sprang up in the same sort of display as Dum's had done, accompanied by frantic beak clicking. He, however, decided not to back away but stood rooted to the spot positively spitting at his prospective breakfast. At last, when the rat was two inches away from his clicking beak, he shrank to half his normal size, put his small tail between his legs and fled to my boot-box and the safety of a cricket boot. However, poor Dee could no longer fit into one cricket boot and all he could do was to put his tail into one and his head into the other.

I sat down flabbergasted, still holding on to the rat, partly because I thought I had frightened them and also because they seemed to be such cowards. Poor little things! They had never seen a rat before in their lives, certainly not such an enormous one as this, so no wonder they were terrified. With a guilty feeling I went into the pantry on my passage and prepared to throw the cause of their terror away. But how could I waste good owl food? Perhaps if it were cut into small pieces they would eat it? I gutted the rat and de-headed and de-tailed it. My nostrils curled at the horrid smell.

Both owls had recovered from their fright when I returned with the two bloody morsels. Dum was again standing on one leg and Dee was walking on the floor, though quite near the refuge of the cricket boots. As I came in they looked at me anxiously, prepared for the worst. I picked them up and placed them on my shoulder as if nothing had happened. I was beginning to get them used to my shoulder. I then put the bed up, covered the wooden surface as usual with paper and placed them both on top. I put the two halves of the rat, cut across the middle of the back, gingerly in front of them. With a hungry yell they fell on their meal of red meat and fur. Both, of course, chose the same piece and a violent tug-o'-war ensued, mingled with grunts and cries from two half-closed beaks. Dum, the bigger, had the advantage of weight but Dee hung on for dear life. The battle raged furiously with a very excited spectator. This way and that went the half-rat, until I suddenly realised there were only two minutes to Chapel.

When I came back to my room at 11.15 at 'Chambers' (Eton jargon for mid-morning break), there were two half-carcasses lying on the bed-top like old, derelict wooden boats with their ribs sticking skywards. Dee and Dum were fast asleep in a corner of the wall. There was also a very angry Dame (matron) waiting to ask what those disgusting-looking objects were and would I remove them instantly as they were liable to spread disease. I agreed with her and wrapped the remains into a parcel and threw it away. I was very relieved as my room stank like a slaughter house.

My Dame was a very tolerant woman and this incident was the only time she ever murmured against Dee and Dum. However, the person who really *was* long-suffering was my Boys' Maid, Miss Siva. Miss Siva is small, very Irish and a hive of activity and adores all things 'wee and sweet', especially young owls. And so the owls had no need for worry from her, although they gave her enough work for four people. She and I agreed how to run the room to suit each other. I was to look after Dee and Dum and she was to clear the room out according to her normal routine. This sounded straightforward, but when every visible inch was covered with newspaper and two owls are in constant moult, clearing out the room became a tricky problem, especially as feathers never seemed to disappear. Miss Siva never once complained and seemed to enjoy doing my room and looking at those 'two old-fashioned professors', as she used to call them. While she cleaned she would talk non-stop to them in Irish. If ever they were to speak, it would have been with an Irish accent.

During her sweepings Miss Siva often had to move them and this they did not like, because she picked them up somewhat roughly and put them to one side. To move them in a gentle fashion would have taken far too long. You had to put your hand just in front of their legs and press up towards the owl's breast. At the same time saying, 'Up.' Both Dee and Dum would take trouble not to overbalance and so when abruptly picked up around the body they naturally objected.

Once Miss Siva came in with a large mop. With a

hungry yell, two fierce owls descended on the woolly head and attacked it ferociously, pulling out long strands with their strong beaks. No amount of shaking would move them and in the end the long-suffering Miss Siva had to pick them up bodily, whereupon they attacked her and actually drew blood. I am afraid they never really liked her after that.

Dee and Dum were always a bit nervous of women, perhaps because they were handled so much by boys. It was not until after a month or so at home that they became attached to my mother, but they would still fly to my father or me for preference.

Other gifts of food I used to receive were boxes of moths and the occasional tender young sparrow. Mice were rare, but when they did come Dee and Dum ate them with relish.

Packets of live moths used to arrive regularly from a boy who caught them in his moth trap. They varied in size from poplar hawk moths to the small, nameless creatures one sees everywhere. They used to arrive by the hundreds in small glass cases, from which I had to remove them with great care as they were eager to escape. Dee and Dum used to eat about thirty or forty at a time when I hand-fed them. I let them eat their fill, because I thought fat moths might contain vitamins and the wings would be good material for the essential pellets. I did not always hand-feed them, but sometimes would encourage the owls to catch them as training for their eventual return to the wild. At first they were afraid of the squirming insects, but soon dashed off in hot pursuit. If they caught one, there would be a frantic fight, with pieces of moth and owl-feathers flying around the room, until the unfortunate insect was swallowed whole. If the moth reached the end of the table first, I would place it back until it was caught.

Sometimes in the moth-boxes there would be a beetle. These, with their hard skin, offered a very different problem. Running the gauntlet would be the same, only the beetles were slower than the moths. The owls found them rather difficult to catch and

even more so to kill, because of their slippery shard of a skin. The fights would be long and fierce and the beetles would often reach the end of the table still game for more, particularly the big cockchafers about an inch long.

One day I had a particularly brave beetle who, when he was halfway along the table, turned round and started to crawl back towards the advancing Dee. Dee stopped dead in his tracks and stared with horror at the advancing beetle. He did not move a muscle and remained rooted to the spot. On came the beetle without hurry or excitement, probing its way with its antennae. It arrived at Dee's right leg. Without altering its pace it climbed up the leg and disappeared into the one-and-a-half inches of fluff which covered the lower part of Dee's abdomen.

Dee had been watching this manoeuvre with fascination, although he had remained quite still. He did not even seem to notice the beetle climbing up his leg. Suddenly, with a convulsive jerk, he sprang at least six inches into the air and landed on his back, pecking and clawing at his stomach. After a few seconds, in a cloud of flying feathers, he managed to seize the beetle plus about fifty of his own feathers and swallowed this mixture immediately, leaving a small bare patch of pink flesh on the right-hand side of his belly. Perhaps the beetle had thought that owl-flesh would be tasty! After this, both owls used to make short work of their beetles, killing them with their talons in seconds.

I had always had great ideas for house-training Dum and Dee but they never materialised. Compared with other birds, like jackdaws, they were not messy,

throwing up their undigested bones and fur in a neat, tidy pellet. The arrival of these pellets was always encouraging, as it showed they were eating the right sort of food. During the first week of their time at Eton the arrival of pellets was awaited anxiously, not only by me but by other boys who were attracted by the characters of the owls. One evening when I was outside my room doing some duty for the welfare of Dee and Dum, I heard a veritable cheer come from my room. This was followed by a patter of feet and a boy, pleasure glowing in his eyes, presented me with a dirty brown object and exclaimed with triumph, 'Dee's sicked up!'

The other kind of mess was a nuisance and all my efforts to make them mess in one corner failed miserably. The room, therefore, had to be covered in paper. When they 'threw a mute', as is the technical term for making a dropping, they would back a couple of feet before doing so. This is obviously a natural instinct to keep the nest clean. But in my room this instinct had disastrous results. For example, if one owl was in the middle of the table facing the wall and felt the call of nature, he would, following his instinct and without looking behind, begin to back, until suddenly he felt thin air beneath him and the hard floor hit him sharply on the behind, three feet below the edge of the table. The owl would then pick himself (or herself) up with a hurt expression, straighten out feathers and relapse into a sulk, in which he or she would remain for at least half an hour. This unfortunate accident left me speechless whenever it happened, and my laughter increased their obvious embarrassment.

On their diet of liver, chick pellets, oil, moths, etc., they flourished, grew and soon began to show signs of genuine flying, not just the flutter and hop, which had been their means of progress after they had learnt to walk. They showed these signs of flying, without warning, by rushing up and down the table or bed-top flapping their wings. This was preliminary and

very soon they were flying from bed to table, table to 'burry' (desk), picture to picture. Dum, being rather aloof, and not so amiable as Dee, would sometimes fly on to the top of the burry, which is the highest point in my room, and spend a great part of the day watching what went on below her with a critical eye.

My room was not very suitable for a novice flyer and there were many accidents. The more frequent was when one of them flew to either the bed-top or the table, which were protected with sheets of newspaper. This newspaper might be sticking out a couple of inches over the edge. And so, after an exhausting flight, the owl seeking the haven of terra firma would put down his feet to land on the nearest part of the table. But no, with an agonising screech and crash the owl would hit the floor. I always felt very sorry for them when I saw their disgruntled faces and ruffled feathers as they picked themselves up.

Another frequent place for landing was my Anglepoise lamp, especially when it was standing straight up. When one landed on the top he or she would have the unpleasant sinking sensation of descending rapidly four or five feet downwards, only to be brought sharply to a halt at the end. If the owl had managed to retain his balance on the lamp part,

he would try to climb up the thin rod. He never succeeded, but just pawed away at the slippery surface trying to get a grip upwards. Neither of them would ever give up until I picked them off.

At this stage they were about eight weeks old and the strong brown feathers of the final plumage were appearing at the roots of the fluff feathers, while the wings and tails had grown enough to allow them to fly. As their flights began to lengthen, I thought I would take them out of doors for exercise.

Exercise time was after six o'clock in the evening on whole schooldays, when I was often free and had no cricket nets.

I would rush into my room, whistling and shouting 'Walkies!' and generally trying to give an impression of excitement. While doing this, I changed out of my tails into 'change' and donned my 'protection'. This was an old rugger zephyr with the front slit open, thus covering my back as I carried my owls sitting on my shoulders, quite free. This was an exhilarating experience as I was terrified they would fly into a tree that I could not climb, and out of which they would not dare to fly as they would be too high.

The exercise walk was always the same; we went over College Field and along the riverbank to Sixth Form Bench, where there is a tree that is fairly easy to climb. Sixth Form Bench is a bench where only members of the Sixth Form are allowed to sit. If anybody else sits there, they are liable to a heavy fine. I am glad to say that Dee and Dum left many traces of their presence.

Once at the tree, which hangs out over the Thames, Dee and Dum would fly into its branches. At first I had to stand close up to the tree to give them confidence, but soon they were flying from ten to fifteen yards to it. When safely in the branches they would hop from branch to branch, revolving their heads at things of interest, climbing up the vertical trunk of the tree with their sharp claws and causing a disturbance among the little birds, who came to mob them. Meanwhile I and another boy, who always came with me in case of trouble, would lie down in the long grass and watch the climbing and flying.

One day when my friend and I were lying on the ground, we noticed that both owls had ceased their usual hopping about and were staring into the long grass a little way away from us. Puzzled, I clambered up the tree and reached Dum, who was the nearest, put my head beside hers and looked in the direction of her glance. Lying in the grass about thirty yards distant was a cuddling couple! I looked at Dum; had her face gone a shade pinker than before?

When it was time to go home, I would have to climb the tree and reach for Dee and Dum with a long stick. They always scrambled further up to the highest branches with a duet of disapproval when they realised that time was up. They disliked the stick I made them sit on intensely and it took much agonising patience to get them down. As I said, this tree overhangs the river and I narrowly missed a ducking many times.

A characteristic of the owls when alarmed at the sight of a dog or a bicyclist on their exercise walks was immediately to go 'thin'. This they did by pressing their feathers as close together as possible and going very stiff while following the object around with their heads. It showed how little flesh and bones they had, and made them appear extremely ugly.

On these outings I'd dig up worms for them, which added variety to their diet. After exercise they would run into a corner, cuddle up together and for three hours sleep the sleep of the exhausted.

At this age also, they began to take an interest in the ground, or really in anything that moved. Undone shoelaces and falling leaves were a great attraction, also paper blown about by the wind and, inevitably, Miss Siva's mop, which had by degrees become much smaller! A great attraction was my pen nib, which they would pounce upon with enthusiasm, an activity they never tired of.

I used to work at my desk with an owl lying on its stomach on each shoulder or perhaps on my lap or arm. When I started to write, their eyes would open slowly and look at the sparkling nib with interest. Perhaps their heads would revolve a little, but very soon the temptation became too great. If they were on my shoulders, they would creep slowly down the whole length of each of my arms on their bellies with their legs pushing and jutting out behind. Dee was an expert at this, but Dum would sometimes roll off and remain suspended under my arm, her claws stuck into my sleeve. When they reached my wrist, they would crouch down, drawing their claws under them, and then with a screech hurl themselves at my nib, pecking and clawing. The resultant blots and smudges all over my work were very annoying. After the amusement of the first assaults, I would jerk my elbow sharply and send them squawking to the ground, where they would sit looking rather sorry for themselves. This never hurt them as they were so light and fluffy. Recovering they would climb up my leg vertically, drawing blood at every step. They never got very far! After a few attempts and after I had shaken them off, Dum would go *Tch, tch* with anger and sulk in the wastepaper basket among the toffee papers and Dee would go to the boot-box, until I paid attention to them again.

When they could fly well, they would just pounce on my nib from my shoulder, spreading ink in every direction and leaving the imprint of their feet clearly on the paper. Masters, not unnaturally, did not approve so I had to restrain them but if it was a letter that I was writing, I just wrote over the imprint, 'Dee sends love' or 'Dum says, "Hello"'. As they were so enthralled with moving objects I soon made them toys of paper balls attached to a piece of string. They chased these with great vigour and on catching them would utter yelps of triumph and begin to tear the paper to pieces with their beaks. This soon developed into tearing all paper into tiny little bits. And so sometimes when I opened the door of my room, clouds of paper and fluff rose and almost obscured everything from sight, like one of those little toys which one shakes and snow falls inside the glass bowl on a tiny model Father Christmas or Christmas tree.

They tore up paper with great deliberation, as if muttering, as they threw the bit on to the floor, 'Take that and that! *And* clear it up.' They did it calmly and rhythmically. Tear with the beak, pause, look at me defiantly, throw it on the floor, tear, look at me, throw it on the floor, and so on until a large pile showed that that day's *Daily Mail* no longer existed.

Swallowing things was another pastime due, I think, to inquisitiveness, with very little regard as to what it was. I had an eye-dropper to give them oil and water, which was about two and a half inches long. One night I could not find it. I retrieved it twenty-four hours later in a pellet. It had been inside one of them, I suspect Dee, for all that time and he had never shown any sign of pain.

One day I came back from school and found Dum, a very fat contented smile on her face, with a piece of string hanging out of her mouth. I gently pulled at the string. Dum grunted and about two inches of string came out, which she immediately tried to reswallow. For the next few minutes I pulled and she grunted, frantically trying to reswallow, until finally I had a three-yard length of string in my hand. No wonder she had looked fat!

A favourite place for exploration was the chimney and one day there was no Dee in sight. After an intensive search I at last looked up the chimney and there, looking down from a ledge two feet up was an anxious face. I pulled out a very, very sooty Dee. This ledge became a frequent happy perch and gave me many a fright, coupled with the added task of giving him a good bath and scrub.

Their curiosity was insatiable. In my room (three yards by seven) there was a window with two casements, both narrow and during the summer permanently open. I never bothered to shut them as the only interest Dee and Dum took in them was to climb the curtains and peer out at the graveyard and cypress trees of College Chapel.

One night I was returning from a play and was walking slowly down the High Street back towards my house when, on glancing up at my window, I felt the hairs on the back of my neck stiffen. There, sitting on the window sill, was Dum!

I ran those last hundred yards in record time, dashed up the stairs, flung open the door and grabbed Dum by the body. I sank on to my bed exhausted, still holding the struggling Dum. You brute, Dum! I thought as I put her down. Dum gave me a reproachful look and pretended to go to sleep.

I undressed, and as I put on my pyjamas, I heard a scraping behind me. I turned around and saw Dum land on the window and crouch in take-off position. 'Dum, stop!' I shouted as I dashed to the window. Too late, and with a look of triumph she disappeared into the darkness of the graveyard and on to a cypress tree.

For a few seconds I stood quite still, thinking words which were better left unspoken. Why had I not shut the window? What could I do at 10.30 p.m. with all the doors locked? Was I going to lose my dear Dum through my own folly? I looked out of the window, but could not pick out any familiar small grey-brown shape.

At last my love for Dum overcame everything else and I decided to find my House Master and ask him for the key to the graveyard. I flung on my dressing gown and slippers and rushed downstairs to his study where I hoped he might still be. I knocked.

'Come in.'

I stood in front of Mr Hill's desk, quite at a loss for what to say.

'Well, what do you want?' he said testily, taking in the scantily clad and dishevelled boy in front of him.

'Well, sir,' I began. 'Well, sir, you see, sir, it all began like this, sir . . .'

'Come on,' he said. 'What is it?'

'One of my owls has flown into the graveyard,' I blurted out.

'Well, what are you going to do about it at this hour of the night?'

'Please, sir, could I have the key of the graveyard, and perhaps I might be able to get him back,' I said hopefully.

Mr Hill looked at me, smiled, and said, 'We can't stand about doing nothing, *let's* go and get her.'

And so saying, with great strides he was past me and out of the door. The last words I heard were, 'Wait by the back door. *I'll* get a ladder and the key.'

As I waited by the back door a thought struck me. Had ever before in the history of Eton a House Master been persuaded at 10.30 at night to rescue a bird, a feathered one?

Just then Mr Hill reappeared carrying a large ladder and the key, and out we went. At first neither of us could see Dum, but at last M'Tutor spied her close to the top of a cypress tree. He put the ladder up but it was too short. By this time several boys were looking out of their windows and one suggested a cobweb mop, which, after a run to the cleaning cupboard on his floor, he handed down. It was at least twelve feet long and just the job.

M'Tutor took it, shinned up the ladder and with the mop hooked the branch Dum was sitting on and pulled it down. As soon as he could reach, he grabbed her with both hands. Dum gave a screech of fury and with all her

strength attacked M'Tutor's hands, who hung on like grim death until he delivered the still scratching Dum into my arms. I looked at his hands and saw blood, much blood! Dum did not stop scratching and biting till we were back in my room. As I was thanking Mr Hill profusely for his noble deed I noticed that a small crowd of spectators had gathered in the road. No wonder! A boy in his pyjamas and a bleeding House Master up a tree at night was no usual sight.

Left: At three weeks
old, they were the
ugliest baby creatures
I had ever seen.

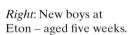

Right: New boys at
Eton – aged five weeks.

Left: Landing, he
would turn fiercely
around and glare out
of his retreat like a dog
guarding its kennel
(eight weeks old).

Top: 'Walkies!' The owls' exercise walk to the riverbank tree, one on each (protected) shoulder.

Bottom left: Early attempts at flying, aged nine weeks. At first I had to stand close up to the tree to give them confidence, but soon they were flying from ten to fifteen yards to it.

Bottom right: When safely in the branches they would hop from branch to branch, revolving their heads at things of interest, climbing up the vertical trunk of the tree with their sharp claws and causing a disturbance among the little birds.

Above: At twelve weeks old. The wings are fully formed now, and the remaining tufts of down slowly giving way to mature feathers, but Dum and Dee are still very obviously babies.

Left: My father met me – in his spotless car. When he saw the colour of my pink protection he refused to let the owls into the car ...

Left: Dee looking simple: she became more of a pet than Dum, who was also more daring and alert than Dee and, I am afraid, far more intelligent.

Right: The daily dip in the birdbath, which they took with great enthusiasm, giving the roses a welcome watering.

Left: Much to the horror of the guests, Dum performed a variety of swoops among the candlesticks and chandeliers.

I had early on wondered whether Dum and Dee were musical – basing this on the awful twanging they made as very young owlets tugging and tweaking at the wire of their cage.

(*Lt-Col. Manning*)

Above left: They would greet me by poking their heads around the edge of the door, one above the other, squawking for breakfast.

Above right: Dee would snuggle closely up against my chest, especially when snow lay on the ground.

Below left: Dee behaved extremely badly, refusing to perch anywhere – though she did consider landing on top of the world . . .   (*Lt-Col. Manning*)

Below right: I thought it would be amusing if Dee were to be sitting on the mascot of my father's beloved Bentley . . . but then I had to spend the next quarter of an hour washing the radiator.

Above left: Every evening at about six o'clock I would go the graveyard to bring Dee home to supper, my heart in my mouth, expecting that perhaps a grave might open up . . . Quite suddenly I would feel something sharp grip my shoulder like the hand of a skeleton . . . Dee's talons.

Above right: Dee with a field mouse. We had succeeded in returning both the owls to the wild able to look after themselves. With their hearing, their eyesight and their silent flight, they are quite different from other birds of prey, and they are masters of the night.

Below: Mouse in sight: I took to placing mice on my chest for Dee to 'catch'. The impact of her pounce was surprisingly painful.

Above: Etonians' plumage, *circa* 1959.

Below: She would sit, fluffing out her feathers, on my shoulder, nibbling occasionally at my ear, which I took for an affectionate caress.

(Lt-Col. Manning)

After this little episode, I kept the windows half-closed and the curtains half-drawn, thus barring any possible further escapades.

Both Dee and Dum were clean-minded and spent much time preening themselves. This was usually done after breakfast and took at least an hour. Each feather was threaded through their beaks several times until the owl was quite satisfied that it lay in its proper place.

To encourage such welcome cleanliness I gave them a bath at least twice a week. The first bath I ever gave them was in the wash bowl in my room. Not unnaturally my room was bespattered with water and I was soaked, so I changed to an ordinary bathtub in the bathroom down the passage. They adored these and could not wait until I had filled the bath with two inches of water, but would try and take a shower under the tap. They would submerge as much as possible under the stream and then shake, scattering the water in every direction. After a bath I didn't let them back into my room for at least half an hour and instead let them dry off perched on the banisters of the stairway.

By the time they left Eton they were fourteen weeks old, much of their final plumage had come through the soft grey feathers and had turned them into a lovely dark chestnut. The head feathers were still not fully formed and they still had grey heads. These grey feathers did not disappear until they were five months old, when they could be considered full-grown.

So much for their daily life at school, now for the Fourth of June.

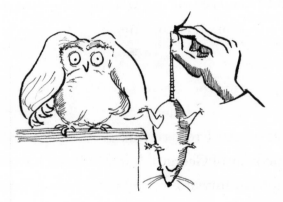

CHAPTER IV

The Fourth of June and Journey Home

Just then, with a wink and a sly normal lurch,
The owl, very gravely, got down from his perch,
Walked round, and regarded his fault-finding critic
(Who thought he was stuffed) with a glance analytic.

JAMES T. FIELDS, 'THE OWL CRITIC'

E VERY YEAR ETON celebrates the Fourth of June, birthday of George III, with a whole holiday. It is a day looked forward to by parents, dreaded by boys and longed for by boys' sisters, especially if they are that year's 'debs', as it gives them a chance to show off their clothes and legs to handsome Etonians! On the Fourth, all parents who possibly can come down, usually in fast expensive cars. My parents are no exception, and my father's car, apart from being fast is also spotlessly clean. I almost have to wipe my feet before getting in.

Mothers and sisters wear clothes of the very latest fashion, and boys wear clean tail suits with flowers in their buttonholes.

On the 3rd I realised that I had somehow to arrange for my owls over the next day, as I could not leave them alone. I knew quite well that I would spend the day walking around with my parents, who would soon find some old friend to chat to, while I would be stranded making polite conversation to my sister.

In the end, I decided that I would have to take Dee and Dum to our picnic lunch . . . in the car. The fatal day arrived and with it my parents, who immediately came up to my room to have a look at Dee and Dum. When they had last seen them, they were the size of tennis balls. My mother was immediately fascinated but my father, without even looking at them, said, 'Phew! This room smells!'

I felt myself boil with rage as I thought of the painstaking trouble Miss Siva and I had taken to make my room respectable. After that I kept a bottle of Airwick in my room but I still refuse to admit that Dee and Dum gave off any unpleasant smell. There was always a faint musty odour but not unpleasant.

After a short owl-worship by my mother and sister, we decided to go and have our picnic. As we were leaving, my father noticed that I had Dee and Dum on my arm.

'Those aren't coming, are they . . . in the car?'

'Oh, yes, they are,' I said, thinking of the taxi driver in Oxford Street.

My father is different from that taxi driver and for the next quarter of an hour we argued. Soon my mother and sister joined in on my side and finally Dee and Dum were allowed to come, on one condition: that they were covered in something. And so poor Dum and Dee had to go through the indignity of being wrapped up in a pair of my pyjamas, one in each sleeve.

My father drove us to the picnic at top speed for fear of being mauled from behind. I was longing to shout, 'Look out! They've escaped!' but thought better of it. We had our picnic beside the river near Runnymede, opposite the historic island. When we were all sitting down, I let Dee and Dum out of their pyjamas. I think they realised that they were left out of the party and with much embarrassment they retired into a clump of reeds, where they disappeared, except for the ends of their tails. They had little peace. Very soon my sister was tempting them with tasty morsels of cold chicken and strawberries and cream in spite of my warning that owls only like raw meat. Nonetheless she went on poking their faces until their moustaches and beards became white with cream. At last Dee bit her and she stopped.

After lunch we returned Dee and Dum to my room, where they sank thankfully into a corner. We then thought we would go to watch the cricket, but hardly had we gone a hundred yards when a friend came up and said, 'Have you got those owls? Please may I come in and see them?'

'Certainly,' I replied. 'In about an hour.'

On we went for another short distance, when again we were approached and asked, 'Please may I come and see your owls?' This went on until six different people had asked and I was becoming more and more worried as I had made appointments for the evening and my father not unnaturally was beginning to wonder if he would ever get any dinner.

Luckily, in the end, only one party turned up to see Dee and Dum. These were a school friend with his mother and sister. His mother is a great friend of my mother and his sister is a lovely debutante. Both were wearing the latest fashion in clothes, one with a large starched hat and the other with a small neat one of chiffon. As soon as they arrived they were captivated by the charms of Dee and Dum and had to be shown how they were kept, fed and how they lived.

'Oh, aren't they heavenly, heavenly creatures.'

'Oh, yes, they're just too, too divine,' they said.

After about quarter of an hour I asked them if they would like to see them having a bath.

'Ooh, yes, please.'

'Well, okay then, come along to the bathroom.'

'Oh, can't they have it here?'

'All right,' I replied, 'but take care, as they are inclined to splash.'

I prepared my wash bowl with a couple of inches of water and placed Dee and Dum on the floor a few inches away.

'They might not be feeling like one,' I said.

A deathly hush spread over the room. Would they or wouldn't they have a bath? Dum looked inquiringly round at the critical faces and then at the bowl of water, towards which she took a few paces. Dee followed. As they came closer to the bath so did the spectators (except me), who were now kneeling on the ground watching every movement.

Dum again looked at the watching faces and then jumped into the basin and stood still.

'Ooh!' gasped the women. Dee sprang in and stood beside his sister. 'Ooh!' again and the watchers drew closer.

Without any warning they started to bathe. Water flew in great splashes in every direction.

The room was filled with squeals, screams and shouts of, 'Mind my hat!' 'Oh, my chiffon, it's collapsed!' 'Oh, my curls!' 'The horrid beasts!'

A few minutes later I was left alone with my sister and Dee and Dum, who were still splashing about as if they were at the seaside. My mother had gone to a cocktail party and my father to a dinner in London. I began clearing the room, with the help of my sister, and drying Dee and Dum who were unusually wet. Very soon the room was respectable, but at that moment my mother came in.

'There is somebody else to see the owls,' she said gaily, 'but don't worry, this one is scared as she was attacked by one once.'

Very cautiously a woman's head appeared around the edge of the door with a frightened expression.

'Oh! How I hate them,' she said, visibly shuddering.

'It's all right, they're sweet,' said my mother.

Dum looked up and saw the frightened face staring at her. Quite innocently, and with an interested look in her eyes, she approached the unknown woman along the table. With a piercing scream the face disappeared and I heard feet echoing down the passage. Dum looked rather shocked and carried on preening herself.

Later on that day my mother surprised me by asking if I would like her to take the owls home. At first I immediately said no, but soon it began to dawn on me that perhaps they were a nuisance and too much of a good thing. I had three hours to think it over. Was my cricket affected? Was my work getting better or worse? I could not decide and for a long time I thought I must send them home. But when I looked at them asleep on the table I felt that parting would be too much and that life would not be the same without them. They stayed.

For the rest of the day I kept them in my room and the only difference from normal was that they went to bed without any protest and fell asleep immediately, worn out by the excitement of their social life.

As the half (i.e. term) progressed, I knew that I should have to take them home either at Long Leave, which is a weekend break two weeks before the end of the half, or at the end of the half. I decided on the Long Leave weekend as Trials (exams) took place during the last week and I had to concentrate.

At first I did not think about the return journey, but when I realised it was only a few days away a number of points struck me. Dee and Dum could not possibly travel in their sleeping cage, as it was too small. This meant they must travel loose on my shoulders, thus calling for some protection for my suit. I needed help and asked a boy, another Jonathan, to help as he lived close by in Suffolk. He immediately accepted and very soon produced two very queer objects, made of flannel, of the brightest pink possible.

'What are those for?' I asked.

'Our protections,' he said gaily holding up two large

rectangular pieces of bright pink cloth with holes in the middle, which I assumed were for our heads.

'We can't wear those,' I said in disgust.

'Why not?' he asked in a hurt tone.

'The colour is too awful for words,' I said, thinking that both our suits were dark in colour, and bright pink cowls would make us look like an exotic branch of the Klu Klux Klan.

'Oh, that doesn't matter, we're looking pretty odd anyway, so why not be completely odd?'

I agreed after some arguing and realised it would not be long before our protections were changed to that proverbial colour, pink with purple spots.

The next problem was how to keep the owls on our shoulders. I knew that they would both sit very tightly and perhaps draw blood with their talons. To satisfy ourselves I made two red leather thongs attached to short pieces of string. These are known as 'jesses' in falconry circles. The leather thong is attached around the bird's leg and thus gives good control to the holder.

I told Jonathan to be careful about these and if, by chance, his owl should fly off his shoulder he must not jerk the string, for fear of dislocating a leg but must play it like a trout with great care.

Windsor Station is a good three-quarters of a mile

away and the risk of Dee or Dum flying free was obvious.

The great day arrived and we donned our pink protections and turned to pick up the owls.

'You pick the liveliest,' said Jonathan, 'as you are the more experienced Owlman.'

I picked up Dee, put his jess on and placed him on my shoulder. Jonathan did the same with Dum. And so with a suitcase in one hand, a cage in the other, an owl on our pink shoulders, and a self-conscious expression on our faces, we walked out of the house.

We walked steadily down the High Street with the jess strings held tightly in our hands, and the reassuring softness of the owls next to our cheeks. We had covered about a hundred yards when suddenly shouts and jeers came from across the street. Other boys going home on leave were using this unusual spectacle for their own enjoyment. I felt the blood rise in my face. I twisted my head and looked at Dee. He had gone slightly 'thin' and had his eyes half-closed, but was regarding the source of noise with complete indifference. I spoke to him and he turned his head and pecked my ear with comforting reassurance.

After about half a mile we reached the end of Eton High Street. I thought that the butcher might like to see what he had been feeding for so long. We went into his shop.

'Look who I have brought to see you,' I said. The butcher looked up, sprang into action and began covering all the visible meat with feverish haste. He soon had everything under cover and turned towards us with sweating brow and a look in his eye which said only, 'Get those things out of here!'

We got out. Neither Dee nor Dum had shown any interest in his sirloins and barons of beef.

We soon reached the station, but not before a lot of people in a bus had leaned out to stare and giggle at us. At Windsor Station a new problem: would we pass the ticket collector and be allowed on the train? Putting on what we thought was a normal expression, we walked firmly towards the booking office. I bought our tickets from a man who just stood and gazed until I asked him to hurry up as the train was about to leave.

Just at that moment I heard Jonathan's voice from behind me, 'Look out, she's gone!' and there he was running for all he was worth down the platform.

'Dum's disappeared into the Ladies' Waiting Room,' he called back over his shoulder. Fearing the worst I dashed after him. Dee, bless his soul, clung on for dear life. A volley of screams confirmed that Dum had indeed flown into the Ladies' Waiting Room. Dum was sitting in the middle of the floor, terrified, while two equally terrified women were edging, with their backs to the wall, towards the door. 'So sorry,' said Jonathan, picking up Dum. We retreated quickly and walked past the ticket collector at top speed. He did not look at our tickets but just gaped. Once in the carriage we shut the door and drew the blinds. So far so good; we were on our way to Waterloo.

Dee and Dum throughout the journey took great interest in the passing landscape. Although our protections had changed colour they behaved themselves quite well and we cleared up any accidents with sheets of paper.

At Waterloo we really did feel nervous for the owls, because the noise that one usually takes for granted seemed greatly magnified and every whistle and shunting, ear-splitting. However, Dee and Dum clung tightly on and looked at everything with more calm than did their master. Apart from the usual crowd there was no disturbance and we hailed a taxi. As the taxi approached it began to slow up, finally stopping about ten yards away. Surprised, we walked over and asked the driver to take us to Liverpool Street Station.

'Not on your life! Not with those bloody things,' he said.

'Please,' I pleaded, putting my hand in my pocket and jingling the contents. 'Oh, all right; hop in, but mind they don't make a mess.' During the drive we realised it would be much more difficult to get on the train at Liverpool Street Station than at Windsor, it being the terminus of one of the main lines. So we thought up a plan and a lie to pull us through: the owls were very valuable specimens and worth a lot of money. We were experienced zoologists taking them to an experimental station. I did not like the thought of Dee and Dum being used for experiments, but there it was.

The taxi stopped and we began to step out. At that moment Dee made a mess on the seat and the taxi driver turned round.

'Who made that mess?' he said.

'I did,' replied Jonathan with a grin on his face and we disappeared into the shelter of the station. On Liverpool Street Station we had no trouble. Dee and Dum decided to be kind to us and remained firmly on our shoulders, although at one moment we were enveloped in funnel smoke as we went over a bridge. We had both ceased to be embarrassed and had let go of the jesses as the birds were behaving so well.

The train officials, in truly British fashion, took no notice of us and we found an empty carriage, very thankful to be on the last lap of the journey home.

Jonathan left me with my two tired companions for an appointment in London. However, I was soon joined by another Etonian. As it was Friday the train was crowded, but even so the carriage remained our own throughout the journey. Occasionally somebody would open the door as if to come in, but quickly shut the door muttering some excuse and hurry away. I offer this as a free suggestion to all those who wish to travel in peace and quiet – just take an owl.

Throughout the journey Dee and Dum slept soundly either on my lap or in between my leg and the corner. Arriving at Saxmundham, a sleepy country market town, the few people there seemed to think that I was mad. But then perhaps I am! My father met me – in his spotless car! When he saw the colour of my pink protection and knew that I had no pyjamas, he refused to let the owls into the car and for a few embarrassing minutes we argued. Finally, we all got in and after a short drive reached our house.

'Home, home!' I shouted with pleasure to Dee and Dum, and all they did was to give me an exhausted look.

CHAPTER V

The Spreading of the Wings

'Hark! Peace! It was the owl that shrieked,
That fatal bellman which gives the stern'st good night.'

WILLIAM SHAKESPEARE, *MACBETH*

THE RECEPTION AT home was very inappropriate for two tired owls. My mother was so glad that they were at last home that she could hardly take her eyes off them for one moment. And so during lunch we put them in the *Pyrus japonica* just outside the dining-room window. Here, for the first few minutes they remained 'thin' but soon were looking at everything with their usual interest, taking special notice of us in the dining room and gazing inquiringly in, especially when anybody laughed.

After lunch we took Dee and Dum to their future roost. This was a small hut with branches for perches, used in the spring for rearing baby chicks, which remained their night-time roost until they were capable of sleeping out of doors.

Throughout the afternoon I popped in to see how they were getting on but they were asleep on one of the perches, or curled up in a corner. They ate very little that night and in the morning were still tired with little appetite. I began to wonder if the journey had been too much for the poor little owls. On the third day Dum began to show signs of recovery and was waiting by the wire door of the hut when I brought their breakfast. Encouraged by Dum's liveliness I took them both out to see their new surroundings. I put them on the rim of a stone birdbath, but neither felt like a bath and Dum soon flew off to the shelter of a small niche in the wall of the house and sat on a bench. Dee was perhaps too exhausted and decided to remain on the rim of the bath. Already many little birds had noticed them and the air was filled with angry chirrups. The swallows were the more daring and took to dive-bombing Dee, who, having never seen a dive-bombing swallow before, was quite overcome. The first swallow which came close to him, made him duck violently and lose his balance. Almost immediately another came straight for him and Dee again tried to get out of the way. Alas, this time with a hurt screech he bit the dust of the rose bed. Poor Dee! I picked him up and placed him beside Dum.

They spent the morning on the bench, going 'thin' at strange objects like cats, dogs and horses. I brought our cat to see them and said firmly, 'No'. Dum and Dee at first went very 'thin' but soon looked as if they would like to make friends. Obviously I disagreed with this prospective friendship and took the eager cat away.

During lunch they again sat on the *Pyrus japonica* and for their lunch I gave them worms. After they had eaten their fill neither knew what to do with the wriggling surplus. But Dum had a brainwave and with a slow step walked to the end of the branch and put them into an empty coconut shell hollowed out by tits during the winter. Dee soon followed suit. Immediately the worms began to climb out and made an extraordinary spectacle with their long bodies waving about over the edge of the nut. Dum did her best to keep them in, but failed.

On the fourth day I had to return to school for the last two weeks of the half and left Dee and Dum in the very capable and affectionate hands of my mother, assisted by the kind help of Susan. I left them with

great sadness in my heart, so wanting to take them back with me. Dum walked about all over me and although it hurt I had not the heart to stop her. Dee, poor thing, was in very bad shape and could only sit on my lap and speak to me in his high-pitched voice. I said goodbye to them in the owl-house, after giving them a mouse each, which they swallowed whole, leaving the tail hanging out of the sides of their mouths. Finally, the tails disappeared down their throats and with a contented look on their faces they fell asleep.

While I was back at school my mother kept a strict routine. After breakfast she would feed them and place them on the bird bath for their daily dip which they took with great enthusiasm, giving the roses a welcome watering with their flapping wings. Dum had a bath first, followed by Dee. In fact, Dum always did everything first and became the more daring of the two.

After the bath they would sit on the edge, waiting for their feathers to dry, as owls are quite incapable of flying with wet wings. All the while the swallows would dive-bomb them. Dum took no notice but Dee still persisted in ducking at each attack. When dry, Dum with a great spring would fly into the mulberry tree about twenty yards away, followed a few minutes later by the more cautious Dee. In the tree, where they would spend the day, they would climb about investigating. There are several trees growing close beside the mulberry and as the owls grew older they would venture into these as well. Dum would explore other trees while Dee went higher and higher. But we had to be careful that they didn't leave for the wild too early, unable to fend for themselves.

Every year our mulberry tree yields a good crop, but last year it exceeded all expectations because Dum and Dee acted as watchmen, scaring off every blackbird and thrush who dared to come near. There was one bird, however, who stayed in spite of Dum and Dee, a little greenfinch, and from dawn till dusk he never stopped squeaking his alarm. He squawked a note, definitely flat, at regular intervals. It became nerve-racking and we all cursed it. My father even threatened to shoot it but my mother was afraid of him hitting Dee or Dum.

In the evenings before dinner my mother and father would fetch the owls, give them their evening meal and put them to bed. This was quite a problem as very often they were a little hesitant about coming down the tree, especially Dee. For the first few weeks Dum would fly to my father in preference, because she was used to men. Later, both became very attached to my mother. On the occasions when they would not come down, they were persuaded by a long pole or hoe with a piece of cloth tied on the end. They hated this pole, above all Dee, who often refused to stay on it. Dum had the good sense to know that at the end of it was a large mouse or rat.

One night Dee decided to remain out, in spite of all calls and whistles. At ten o'clock my mother, very worried, left him to the horrors of the night. These are many and come in the shape of wild owls which abound in our garden. Owls, like many birds, have 'territories' and if other owls do not respect boundaries, they are driven out by force. And so poor Dee spent a night in the wild. In the morning a very anxious face was waiting on the bottom branch of the mulberry tree. He flew to my mother's arms quacking with joy; even so it was only a week before he spent another night out. About this time I returned from school. I went straight to the mulberry tree. I could not see them anywhere and hard as I looked I could only detect green leaves. Something whizzed by my ear and a white patch appeared on the path at my feet. I looked up and there was Dum's tail. I called with pleasure, 'Dum, it's me!' She clicked her beak and ignored me. Calling and whistling I found Dee and managed to get them both down. In our old nursery, I put them down and gazed at them with rapture.

They had changed so much; not just in growth but in general appearance. Dum was much bigger and lighter in colour and her feathers had grown far more than Dee's. They were both very lively, Dum especially, who strode around the room squawking at the top of her voice. Her voice had also changed and it was now harsh and raucous as if broken. I hoped she would soon hoot. Dee's, however, had become shrill and high-pitched and he wasn't so interested in things as Dum.

The tone of their voices made me wonder if I had guessed their sexes right, and the more I thought of it the more I came to the conclusion I was wrong. Another thing which made me wonder about this was the differences in the colour of their faces. Somewhere I had read that female owls' faces had a more rufous tinge than males'. Dee's face certainly was more 'rufous', while Dum's had taken on a somewhat white colour with a growing white moustache, which in two months' time was magnificent. Dum was also more daring and alert than Dee and, I am afraid, far more intelligent. I soon noticed that.

The door of their 'house' is made of wire. Dum never tried to get through it, but one day my sister found Dee hanging by his beak near the top, half dead, having flown against the wire. Dum would never do that. But neither of them appreciated or understood glass and would bang their heads against it.

After much thought, their sexes changed in my mind, and Dum became 'he' and Dee 'she'. This has remained so ever since. Also with this change, the affections of my mother and myself altered. Dum ceased to be a pet, but instead we admired and loved him with respect. Dee became more of a pet, and I loved her with more affection than I have felt for any other animal apart from Dum.

Their food was becoming more and more natural.

We fed them twice a day and usually with mice, sparrows or rats, which were caught skilfully by 'Brad' Balls, who looks after our horses and helps in the garden. He is an expert at trapping and also at spearing rats with a pitchfork as they run across the stable. On an average I got about three rats every two days. These I had to cut up as the owls' beaks were not yet strong enough. But with young sparrows and mice, quick and clean, they swallowed them whole. At first I gave these to them dead, but once I brought them two newly-hatched sparrow fledglings. Dum and Dee were amazed that their breakfast actually moved. Finally, Dum with a determined look sprang on top of his and immediately killed it with his talons, which were by now long and sharp. It was horrid to watch, but nature is 'red in tooth and claw'.

Sometimes I gave them worms covered with feathers, which crawled across the table like some strange caterpillars. Although this diet sounds well balanced, it was not quite sufficient and they still needed liver. With an eye-dropper, we squirted halibut oil down their throats every day.

The day I dreaded soon arrived, the start of encouraging them to return to the wild and freedom. Until now they had spent the night in, and the day out. It came one night about a week after my return from school when Dee refused to come down from her tree. After much worried calling we decided to leave Dum out as well to keep her company and so with anxious hearts we went indoors and left them out all alone.

I went to my bedroom and opened the window. The night air was full of hoots and screams as if every owl in the neighbourhood had come to visit our garden. In two large cedar trees I counted eight wild owls apart from our two. Above this discordant chorus I could just make out Dee's high-pitched squeak and Dum's raucous squawks. Why won't they keep quiet? I thought. They will only attract attention and perhaps there will be a fight and they will be killed.

I slept very little that night, kept awake by Dee and my own nerves. At the first streak of dawn I rushed out into the garden and whistled. There was no answer and a terrible apparition of Dum torn to pieces came before my eyes. I whistled again. A loud squeak just beside me made me start. There was Dee sitting on a low branch. She hopped on to my arm and walked up to my shoulder. Just then I heard Dum's raucous voice from about a hundred yards away and there he was flying towards me. I ran to meet him and with a volume of harsh quacks he landed on my other shoulder.

When I had them both safely back in the nursery and was giving them breakfast, I noticed Dum had changed. He was still just as tame but he strutted about with a pride and self-confidence that made me think that the day for his departure was near. Dee, however, was still the same and just as simple-minded.

After about two weeks of the holidays I went away for several days leaving arrangements for the upkeep of Dum and Dee. When I came back the rats and mice had run out, due to my negligence, and consequently they were fed on the very inadequate food of horsemeat. Why it had changed from liver, I do not know.

One day Dee fell over when she was walking across the table, and she could hardly pick herself up. Dum also was a bit lame but I put this down to accidents. The next day I could not find Dee in the mulberry tree. Finally, I heard her faint squeak and there she was lying on the ground. I tried to pick her up but she screamed and pecked at my hands. I carried her to the nursery, where she could only lie on the table and whimper pitifully. She was in agony, poor thing. Then it dawned on me that both owls had got what I had fought against and dreaded ever since that April morning of their arrival. They were suffering from a spreading paralysis due to lack of vitamins.

I turned the nursery into Dee's sick room and put her on some blankets. Dum only had a slightly bad leg so I left him outside. The next day Dee was far worse and could only just move her head. That day I stuffed her with mice, sparrows, and halibut oil, but the next day she was almost dead. My mother expected her to die, so did I, so did we all, and life became gloomy.

In desperation my mother rang up Dr Garnet, our local doctor, and asked if he had anything to fight off paralysis. He is a great authority on birds and keeps ornamental ducks on his pond. He sent out an oil called Abidec, containing at least six vitamins. We gave Dee an extra dose and went to bed, knowing that the morning would bring either death, which was the more probable, or recovery.

In the morning Dee was still alive, but only just and barely managed to open her eyes and beak for a piece of Abidec-saturated sparrow. The next day she was still only just alive. On the sixth day after she fell ill, she managed to move her head and squeak for her meals. After a week of slow recovery she was out of danger and life for all was bearable again. Throughout her illness she never lost her appetite.

As soon as we could, we picked her up without hurting her. My mother or I would nurse her on our laps, especially at tennis parties, where she would watch the balls flying back and forth over the net. This gave her neck good exercise so we always took her to watch hoping that it would help her recovery.

While Dee had been at death's door, Dum had got over his bad leg with the help of the Abidec and was just the same as ever. He had taken to putting food into his mouth with his talons instead of pecking it off the ground. It was rather uncanny and rather human.

One night, when Dee was recovering, I went out to give Dum his evening meal at about eight o'clock. As usual he was delighted to see me and came to sit on my shoulder. Just at that moment I heard a very queer owl-hoot from a tree a few yards away and the shape of an owl flew across the lawn. Dum's talon bit into my shoulder, which I took to be a reaction of fear, but with a loud quack he flew after the wild owl. I expected to hear the sounds of a fight but, no, there was complete silence.

I went back into the house wondering what this meant. The following evening Dum flew to me with his usual loquacious greeting but I noticed that he was a little nervous and eager to be off. As I was giving him his last piece of rat, there came the same weird hoot from the cedar tree, as if the hooting owl's mouth was full of water, and again the shape of an owl flew across the lawn. Dum immediately followed and soon caught up and thus, wing-tip to wing-tip, they disappeared into the darkness. It was obvious what had happened; Dum had found his heart's desire and preferred her to me. I went to bed that night rather sad and wrapped up Dee in her sick bed with greater tenderness than usual.

It soon became a nightly sight to see the wild owl waiting for Dum, who had the same regular nocturnal habits as Cupid visiting Psyche. In the morning Dum was always waiting for me in the mulberry tree, there being no sign of the wild owl at that time of day. Soon the wild owl became bolder and used to sit on one of the chimney pots waiting for Dum. I hated this owl at first, with its weird hoot, and was sorely tempted to shoot it on the chimney right then and there. Why should it come and take away my Dum after all my trouble? Was this justice? But I suppose it is natural for owls to fall in love, just as it is for us humans, and I accepted it after a struggle. Dum was overjoyed when he heard the hoot and would quack with excitement. Dee, however, as soon as she heard another owl or saw one, would go 'thin' and silent and stop her conversational squeak. This was one of their great differences.

After two weeks of convalescence Dee was allowed into the tree again during the daytime. I couldn't find her the first time I went to look for her. I searched and searched fearing that she might have been eaten by a cat. At last I found her on the ground where she had fallen due to the weakness of her legs. Time and time again she fell to the ground, where she would lie helpless, an easy prey.

One day I opened the nursery door and saw the tail of our cat protruding from the edge of the flower border. At the same time I heard the cracking of bone between strong teeth and thought our cat was devouring another rabbit. But I noticed a few grey feathers striped with brown on the ground beside the cat. For a full moment I stood stock still and then, with red before my eyes and with a sob of rage, I hurled myself at the murderous cat.

The feathers, the bones, the corpse, were those of a young pheasant!

On the whole we had little trouble from the cats, who at the first meeting were certainly more frightened than the owls themselves. Even so, one day Dum had a

narrow escape. My mother was feeding him in the mulberry tree. As she finished, she noticed the head of a cat, in the fork of the branches, five yards from the unsuspecting Dum. With his body pressed down the cat shot along the branch with murder in his eyes. Dum saw him in the nick of time and with a squawk flew away. My mother, a tennis player, delivered a smashing forehand and the cat flew through the air to land on the ground a good five yards away. There, he picked himself up and fled as if all the furies in hell were after him.

By now, Dee was almost her old self and one afternoon I took her up to bed with me to have a rest. I put her beside my shoulder where she happily went to sleep. When I was almost asleep I suddenly felt a creeping object on my cheek. I swatted it, but it remained there. I swatted it again but it still carried on crawling across my face. I pinched it between my nails. It was a louse. Poor Dee during her illness had had no chance to keep herself clean. We called the vet and with some powder the lice were soon cleared up. Dee now looked much healthier and her feathers took on a new sheen.

A few days after we let Dee out into the mulberry tree again, we couldn't find her anywhere. After searching for an hour, I gave up. The next day there was still no sign of her and we all expected her to be dead. Then something extraordinary happened. On the third night, with Dum on my shoulder, I went out and called for her. Dum squawked and quacked. It was a still night without a breath of wind and the air smelt heavily of cedar sap. Suddenly Dum went silent and I felt his talons dig into my shoulder. Then I heard far, far away a very faint squeak. Dum flew into the nearest tree and began to squawk with great enthusiasm. Then he went silent again while an answering squeak came from the direction of a farmhouse some 200 yards away. With a look at me Dum flew off to the next tree in line with the farm. There he stopped and squawked. Again the faint squeak over the soft summer's air. Off Dum went to the next tree while I followed as best I could over fence and gate.

The squeak became louder and louder until finally I reached the farmhouse, and there was Dee sitting on a wall in the farm's garden calling plaintively. I rang the bell of the house and asked the farmer, Mr May, if I could retrieve my owl from his garden. (He is, incidentally, the uncle of that brilliant cricketer, Peter May.)

Both he and his wife came out to see Dee, and as we approached, we could see her lonely pathetic expression, whilst Dum with a great quack of triumph flew low over our heads and circled above.

Dee was delighted to see me and snuggled up when I put her inside my sweater. I looked up at the circling Dum and inwardly thanked him for finding Dee, but just at that moment there came that usual inviting hoot and off he flew off into the darkness for his nightly date.

Dum's help astounded me, as he had never shown any affection for his sister. But that night he had certainly led me to her. Perhaps he did it to help me or perhaps he knew how much I loved him and his sister and tried to return such affection. I hope so, and I like to think that he did it for that reason.

The next night Dum was missing and so was the wild owl. I felt I had seen him for the last time and his help of the previous night was his farewell gesture. I was resigned and went about thinking of the happiness I hoped he was enjoying.

Three days later it was my birthday and who should turn up at lunchtime but Dum. I was walking past our grass tennis court when I heard a joyous quack and there was Dum, handsome and lively as ever, wishing me a happy birthday. His moustache and eyebrows were whiter and more dashing; a contrast to Dee's gentle russet face. But that night the wild owl turned up as usual and off they flew side by side.

During the next week both Dee and Dum became more friendly than usual. They were always pleased to see my mother and me when waiting to be brought in. And going into the garden, I only had to whistle and an answering squawk or squeak always came back. They did, however, show some discrimination about answering to any old person. Once, I brought some friends to see them, who were dressed in gaudy clothes and chattering at the top of their voices. I scoured the garden whistling but answer came there none.

The visitors left disappointed and I walked back to the house under the cedar trees. As I passed under the cedar nearest the house, I heard a very soft *kwee* beside my ear. There was Dum sitting on the lowest branch of a tree, under which only a few moments before I had been calling for him.

Often they could be too pressing. In the mornings they were either waiting at the nursery windows or they'd waddle into the house of their own accord, when the front door was opened. This was not popular, as they always took the first turning to the left and this happens to be my father's study and is as sacred as his car. They would greet him by poking their heads around the edge of the door, one above the other, squawking for breakfast.

Apart from walking in at the front door, they would occasionally fly in through an open window, especially when it was getting dark. One night we were having dinner, when suddenly with a loud quack Dum landed on the open window sash and looked down at us with disdain, like an Assize judge about to pass sentence of death. 'Hello, Dum,' I said cheerfully. Dum's face lit up. My father's comment, 'That owl is not coming in here,' somewhat dampened our enthusiasm.

Dum had different ideas and with half a hoot swept

down among the candles, seized the grapes my mother was about to eat in his talons, and disappeared into the outer darkness with a shriek of triumph. I wonder if he enjoyed his dessert.

Another occasion of a similar sort was at a formal dinner party. Without any warning two loud thuds came from the windows, still unshuttered as it was summer. All the guests started in their chairs. Parading up and down on the window sills at ground level outside were my two owls, every now and then banging the panes with their beaks. They did this with perfect discipline.

The two tall windows are side by side, only separated by a foot of wall. Dee and Dum began a sort of dance starting from the middle when only a foot away from each other. First, they would tap the window and then walk sedately crabwise to the far end where again they would stop and bang the pane, immediately walking back inwards again. It was done with such precision that the bangs almost came together and in step. They reminded me of the Bisto Kids.

This parade lasted for a couple of minutes until Dum disappeared, only to fly into the dining room with several loquacious quacks. Here, much to the horror of the guests, he performed a variety of swoops among the candlesticks and chandeliers, almost blowing the candles out. At the end of these acrobatics, both owls disappeared into the darkness of the nearby trees.

Throughout this flying display, there had been a deathly silence except for a 'Aren't they divine?!' from my sister, only to be quickly silenced by the solemn atmosphere. But at the end there was a noticeable sniff as the guests resumed their dinner. I felt rather hot under the collar but managed to wink at my mother.

Although they were friendly to me, they were most unpleasant to each other and were forever squabbling and fighting. Often when my mother held out her bare arm for them to alight upon, they would both land together and begin to fight for possession. One

can imagine the state of a delicate, bare arm after two owls have been fighting on it.

My mother not unnaturally didn't like this at all, and even thought of trying to get rid of one and keep the other as a permanent pet. We had been training them to find their own living, because I thought that with my eventual departure from home it was essential that they returned to the wild as soon as possible. Also, when my parents were away, there was only Susan to look after them and she had to go back to school as well.

I started to teach them by tying a mouse to a piece of string and dragging it across the floor, enticing the owls to chase it. They very soon learnt and it became quite a sport to try to keep the mouse from their clutches. A more advanced lesson was to catch a mouse alive in a special trap, put it in a circular horse-feed tin and place tin and prospective dinner under where the owls were perching. At first, they just stared down, moving their heads round and round.

'Go on, you two, it's for real,' I would say and prod the unfortunate mouse to make it move.

Dum pounced first of course and landed beside the mouse. To begin with, he just stood still watching the mouse. When the mouse moved, he grabbed it in one talon and pecked at it before killing it with an extra squeeze. He flew off to swallow it in the rafters above. Dee followed with the next mouse and they were on their way to becoming skilled hunters.

My mother tried to give Dee away, as she liked Dum the best for his dominating character. I was away and had little say in the matter, but I was heartbroken to hear of this. However, she failed, thanks to a remark made by the brother of the girl who was going to have Dee. He said, 'It won't be an 'owling success,' so the girl's parents quite rightly objected, and Dee stayed with us.

For returning to the wild, we decided it would be a good idea to ring them in case they strayed and someone found them. My mother wrote to the Natural History Museum to ask for details. The answer was brief. It said that on no account were birds to be ringed by people inexperienced with birds and that as soon as the owls had complete freedom they would inevitably die. I tore the letter up in disgust.

A few days later, we decided to keep both owls for a little longer to make sure of their training but, as if in retaliation, Dee thought otherwise and disappeared for the day. She was now quite healthy. One evening my sister was clearing out the stables and Dee was watching her with her usual curious simple manner when she noticed a young swallow about to fly sitting on the stable door. With a triumphant shriek she swooped down, seized the unfortunate swallow in her talons and flew off into the garden. My sister, overflowing with compassion, rushed out of the stables brandishing the stable broom and cursing Dee for her bloodthirstiness.

That was the last I saw of Dee those holidays, in spite of the many heartbreaking hours I spent calling and whistling. Oh dear, had she gone for ever?

I contented myself with the thought that Dum, in spite of his love affair, was still with me. He was growing more handsome and more mature every day and it was at this time I saw him hoot for the first time. He was sitting on the wall just outside our old nursery one evening, when I went to feed him. As I stood below him the wild owl flew up from behind and settled on one of the chimneys. Then it hooted its hoarse, unearthly cry. I looked at Dum. He was watching. Very slowly he looked at me and then began to puff his chest out to twice its normal size. Once more he looked at me and then he uttered a very short *Twoo-hoo*. Maybe as a result of so much effort, he suddenly shrank to half his size and glanced quickly back at me. Then with rapid strides he tiptoed to the end of the wall without a backward glance. Poor Dum was obviously embarrassed by his first attempt at adulthood!

A few days later some friends of my parents were staying and it was not until after dinner that my mother remembered that she hadn't shown them the owls. In order to get the utmost dramatic effect she decided not to show them in the usual way but to wait until it was dark. Then she said casually, 'Would you like me to conjure up the spirits of the night?'

'What do you mean?' they said.

'You'll see,' said my mother and walked out into the garden through the French windows. She raised her arm and whistled into the surrounding gloom. The only sound that could be heard was the sighing of the wind among the cedar boughs. The two onlookers waited expectantly a few feet from my mother's arm.

Without any sound or warning, Dum, with his white face, was sitting on my mother's arm looking exactly like a ghost. He, as all owls do, had flown absolutely silently across the lawn.

With a piercing scream the woman fled into the house and peered anxiously out of the window.

'It's all right, he's sweet, he won't come in,' said my

mother. Dum thought differently and glided gracefully into the drawing room, circled the chandelier, settled on a large bookcase, gave a loud hoot and surveyed the room with interest.

'Ooh,' gasped the woman, 'I hate all feathered birds,' and left the room on winged feet.

Dum cocked his ears at the slam of the door, gave another hoot and flew out again.

By this time the holidays were coming to an end and there were only a few days left. I began to make plans for the upkeep of Dum while I was away. One morning I went out to call for him. There was no answer. No answer! This was the first time there had been no answer for two weeks.

I spent the day whistling and calling near every tree I had known him to occupy. In the evening there was still no sign of him nor was there any wild owl waiting. I was worried and slept little for the next few nights, and spent the time listening to other owls calling outside my window, hoping to hear Dum's own hoot.

The day for return to school arrived. I spent the morning scouring the countryside on my horse, stopping and calling for Dee and Dum at every hollow tree. But no reassuring quack or squeak answered my plaintive calls. I went back to school that afternoon depressed beyond words and resigned that I would never see either Dee or Dum again. The Natural History Museum was right, after all; they had perished.

CHAPTER VI

Return to Nature

A falcon towering in her pride of place was by a
mousing owl hawked at and killed.

WILLIAM SHAKESPEARE, *MACBETH*

When I reached school I tried to make myself forget the owls by convincing myself that they had been too much of a nuisance and that I was well rid of them. However, after a week or so, I was writing home asking if there had been any sign of Dee or Dum. The answer was always no, and I slowly became accustomed to the idea of them in the wild.

When I had been at school for three weeks I, very inconveniently, developed acute appendicitis and came home for two weeks after the operation. I spent the first week convalescing and wandering about on the off-chance of hearing or seeing Dee or Dum. My searchings were fruitless.

One day, my mother rang up Mrs May about some flowers and at the end of the conversation Mrs May happened to remark on the quantity of owls around her farmhouse.

'One has taken up residence in one of the barns,' she said, 'and I was wondering if it's one of yours.'

My mother put the telephone down and called for me. We walked down at top speed. On our arrival, Mrs May told us that she had seen, rather surprisingly during the day, an owl in a clump of low trees near the barn. I went to the copse and whistled. I heard a very faint squeak which stimulated my searchings. Then a squeak close by. I turned, and on a low branch was Dee!

'Dee!' I cried out with pleasure. She ruffled her feathers and squeaked. I put her inside my coat and went home walking on air.

I went straight into the nursery, sat down, put her on my wrist and gazed at her. The sight that met my eyes was horrible. How she had changed! She was emaciated, half her previous size and weighed next to nothing. She could barely stand up and her eyelids were half closed. She was nearly dead.

I immediately gave her a small meal of liver and a dose of Abidec, which she devoured ravenously. I gave her no more right then for fear of overloading her obviously shrunken stomach.

That night she threw up a pellet. I broke it up to see what she had been eating during her six weeks' absence. It was a pellet of starvation, containing sycamore seeds, grass and leaves, but no bones or fur. How she had survived is still a mystery to me. Perhaps Artemis, that goddess of forests and hunting, had lent a hand.

Dee soon recovered and was her normal self again. Three nights later she was sitting on the wall outside the nursery waiting to be fed. Suddenly there was a loquacious quack, and Dum was beside her and striding up and down the wall. Dee flew into the nursery and settled on a radiator squeaking for her supper. Dum followed and perched beside her. What a fabulous sight! How lovely they were together, yet so different in appearance and character. With their flat faces and large eyes, they looked more human than other birds. Both of them could swivel their heads through well over 180 degrees. Dum was now full grown and much taller and more imposing than Dee. Proudly he strutted about as if he owned the place. When he looked at me with his large brown eyes, I felt rather small. His moustache and whiskers were long and white. However, he was still tame but rather nervous of being stroked and being within four walls. He was, truly, a perfect specimen of a tawny owl.

I was so pleased that they had both returned that I was only capable of staring with rapture at them on the radiator.

While I was watching, Dum suddenly turned and strode rapidly towards Dee, clicking his beak. I wondered what was going to happen and watched with interest, hoping that they might be slightly attached to each other.

Without any warning Dum threw himself at Dee, spitting and clicking.

Poor Dee was shattered by this sudden onslaught but bravely fought back. Thus I became, in a very few seconds, an eyewitness of an owl fight.

An owl fight is like no other fight. It is the most horrible I have witnessed; forget schoolboy boxing. The phrase 'No holds barred' would be an understatement. They used their talons with as much ferocity as their beaks and their wings for balance and hitting-power.

They fell to the ground with an ear-splitting screech and proceeded to do their best to kill each other. Dee, owing to her size and bad health, was soon on her back

and would have been killed if I had not separated, at the cost of much blood, the two fighters.

All this happened so swiftly that I had only reacted when I realised that Dee's life was in danger.

As soon as I had separated them, Dum, with a hoot of triumph mixed with disgust, flew out of the open door to his waiting friend in the mulberry tree.

One would naturally deduce from this battle that Dum and Dee hated each other, but as the months passed it became obvious that there was still a little friendship left. For instance, if I wanted to see Dum or hear him – he was now completely independent of us – I only had to wait for a calm still night and make Dee squeak loudly. If she kept it up long enough, I would hear Dum's clear cry and the wild owl's full-bodied hoot. Then in perfect formation, an envy to any fighter squadron, they would fly across the winter's moon. I seldom did this because seeing Dum brought back too many happy memories and such nostalgia for those wonderful days together. But I did feel proud that we had successfully nursed and helped him back into the wild. When Dum or the wild owl called, Dee would go quite silent and 'thin' and remain so until we got home. She always went thin, and still does, when she hears another owl.

When Dee recovered her full health, she went back to the farm, from where we had to fetch her every night to be fed, carrying her under my mother's coat or in my sweater. Like this she became quite relaxed and would snuggle closely up against our chests especially when snow lay on the ground. These were some of the rare occasions when she ever showed any affection.

But she did continue to stay down at the farm and had to be fetched every night, which became slightly tedious. It seemed as if there was only one-way traffic among the owls on this route. I never minded fetching her from the farm barns, but when she took up abode in the churchyard cypress I did begin to object.

Our church dates from the fourteenth century and has some ancient gravestones. It is also perched on top of a hill, surrounded by tall pines and ivy-covered oaks. By the side of the church there is a clump of cypress trees. Dee took up residence in one of these during December.

Every evening at about six o'clock I would go to bring her home to supper. If I arrived before time she would only squeak and refuse to come down. Some nights the wind would howl round the church and the moon's rays from behind the pines would be hidden by scudding clouds. I would walk carefully among the gravestones, with my heart in my mouth, expecting that perhaps a grave might open up, exposing its ghastly contents.

Quite suddenly I would feel something sharp grip my shoulder like the hand of a skeleton. I would stand stock still, feeling probably like the miser in M. R. James's ghost story 'There Was a Man Dwelt by a Churchyard'. Dee had arrived in her usual complete silence. No wonder I objected! Who would not?

A favourite perch of hers after dark was an old ivy-covered cross. She also took great pleasure in flitting from gravestone to gravestone. Scared? Me? Of course not. Well . . .

I had always had ambitions to train my owls to sit on my shoulder while I rode a horse or bicycle like a horseman from Outer Mongolia. Both these ideas failed miserably. I had only gone five yards on my bicycle when Dee flew off. I never tried that again or on a horse. I had left it too late.

Weeks passed with their usual speed, and Dee still remained in the cypress trees while we occasionally heard Dum. Everybody realised with regret that we had seen the last of him.

Thus ended the year 1959, and the new year began with its unknown future for man and bird alike.

Dee celebrated the new year by flying back from the churchyard to our coach house, where she took up permanent residence in a small harness room at the side with the window and main door left open. We feed her at sundown and she spends the night out. Sometimes she does not return for a week or more but visits neighbouring farms, where no doubt she sits on haystacks catching mice. For some extraordinary reason she always comes home on a Friday night.

RETURN TO NATURE

One day I decided to take Dee to a professional photographer, Colonel Manning, a man of great patience, who has now photographed everything from a fierce owl to a squalling baby. He does not, however, have as much hair as he used to have. Dee behaved extremely badly, refusing to perch anywhere except on our defenceless heads. Poor Colonel Manning's head was streaked with blood at the end of the session. Still, the photographs were a success thanks to his skill and cunning.

I also tried to photograph Dee myself and I thought it would be amusing if she were to be sitting on the mascot of the 'sacred' car. Reckoning that my father might not co-operate, I stealthily pushed it out of the garage.

I put Dee on the mascot. My sister came to help. The cameras clicked and there were exclamations of 'Clever girl', 'Good girl'. But just then I saw something that made me gasp. I hardly dared look. The biggest and blackest mess was sliding down the silvery radiator. I spent the next quarter of an hour washing the radiator while continually looking over my shoulder, fearing at any moment to see my father striding round the corner!

Just before Christmas, when my father wasn't feeling

too well, I took Dee into the drawing room to cheer him up.

'Here's Dee to see you, Daddy,' I said gaily.

'Don't let her fly off, will you, now.'

'Oh, no!'

Dee immediately took off, circled the room and then quite deliberately flew about six inches away from the mantelpiece. She created such an airstream that all the Christmas cards fell off. I removed her for the greater safety of myself and the drawing room.

One day I walked into the coach house to feed her but she refused everything I offered. I felt slightly worried but noticed a pile of black feathers in a corner.

'Oh, Dee, you cad, you've had a blackbird.' I kept it to myself, not wishing to arouse the feelings of the household against her.

This was not the last of her kills. A few days later she had a robin, and then a sparrow. She can be excused these murders though, because these birds used to come into her harness room to eat the horses' corn. What will happen when the swallows return this year is too awful to contemplate. She used to keep these kills in an old basket. Once when I went to have a look and before I could touch the basket, Dee threw herself at me with a screech of anger. I got very badly scratched and as a result have never tried to look again.

On another occasion in early spring, I went into the coach house to do some work and heard an extraordinary noise. It made me stand quite still. It was a low 'coo', somewhat like a turtle dove, but more musical. I walked towards its source, which was Dee's room. There, sitting on her perch with her throat swollen, was Dee singing to her heart's content. I sat down and listened enraptured. It was beautiful! I suppose it is the female owl's mating call. She is not a fully developed female yet and is very small, I am sure due to the terrible disease she contracted. I have been trying to remedy this by giving her female hormones which I thought might act in two ways. One, to develop her female instincts, and, two, to make her more subdued and tractable, because her periods of absence, alas, are becoming longer and more frequent.

In some ways they have worked. She now spends a great deal of her time in the coach house loft sitting on a nest-box made for her. She coos that lovely coo and hoots at every person who comes in.

One night a few days ago I went into the loft to collect some straw. With a screech of fury Dee attacked me, so perhaps she is thinking of making a nest.

It's mid-April now and I have to return to school. Yesterday I realised that it was a year ago to the day that the owls came into my life. I went into the coach house, where I was greeted by the usual fully developed hoot. Dee was so pleased to see me that she could not sit still. She snuggled up under my sweater and I took her into the nursery and fed her. After she had had enough, I put her on my shoulder and we went for a walk around the garden.

The evening was calm and without a breath of wind. I felt happy and pressed my cheek against Dee who I hope felt happy too.

We were passing the cedar trees when with his clear hoot Dum and his friend flew over our heads and settled on an upper branch. I looked up at him in the tree and then at Dee on my shoulder. Both were one year old and yet so different. Where would Dee be this time next year? Perhaps still with me. Perhaps gone back to the wild. Perhaps with babies. Who knows?

I turned around and Dee and I returned to the coach house. I could not have been happier.

NOVEMBER 1960

CHAPTER VII

Aftermath: Dee Dee

St Agnes' Eve – Ah, bitter chill it was!
The owl, for all his feathers, was a-cold.

JOHN KEATS, 'THE EVE OF ST AGNES'

'DD HAS RETURNED, please telephone immediately.'
What on earth does that mean? I wondered, sinking painfully into my chair after a rough game of football and letting the piece of paper fall to the ground.

I stretched my legs and sank further into my armchair, looking forward to the hot bath waiting down the passage.

Life was good; 14 November and the publication day of this book about Dee and Dum. Football was tiring but satisfying. I was quite content lying in my chair thinking of nothing.

'DD has returned.' The message seemed even odder as I read it again to see who'd sent it. The signature was that of the M'Dame, the House Matron, which meant that it was not a school message, but probably from home. From home!?

I sat up with a jerk, realising in a split second what a fool I was.

DD, of course, meant Dee Dee, I said to myself. 'Dee Dee is my mother's pet name for *Dee*! Dee my tame owl whom I had last seen in April, Dee whom I had nourished from a blind three-week-old owlet, Dee whose sudden departure seven months before had been like losing a trusted friend and whose return was like that of the prodigal son, except that she had done no wrong.

I ran to the matron's room, regardless of my semi-nudity, in search of a telephone. All ideas of publication day, football and a hot bath were driven from my mind at the thought of Dee remaining faithful to me after so long in the wild.

I felt supremely happy even though the telephone operator took an unbearable length of time to get through to our home number, but soon I heard my mother's voice at the other end. She told me what had happened.

Brad, had, as usual, gone into the coach house to give the horses their morning feed, when he heard an unusual clacking noise in the loft above. At first he took no notice, but when it happened again a few minutes later he climbed the ladder to investigate.

The result was obvious and he immediately fetched my mother who rushed over full of excitement. Not wanting to climb the ladder, she stood at the bottom and whistled as she and I had whistled so often. There was an answering squeak and the next second Dee was on her shoulder demanding loudly to be fed as if nothing had happened in all those seven months she'd been away.

My mother fed her with liver and feathers, which she ate ravenously. During the meal Dee walked over my mother's arms, shoulders and head, all the time squawking and beak-clicking. It seemed she was glad to be home and was treating my mother to a relieved-to-be-home greeting. My mother had difficulty getting her to leave her arm as she put her in the old harness room. She shut the door to keep her safe until I came home at the beginning of December. It was then that my mother left a message with the matron, who had simply written down the letters 'DD'.

During the next month Dee was extremely friendly

and did not object to her confinement in the harness room at all, and amused herself hooting at everybody who came in.

Her hoot had changed from the short one-note hoot of seven months before, to a long quavering, slightly threatening, cry. This gave her some privacy especially from four-footed animals such as cats.

Although Dee seemed happy in the coach house, there was another member of the owl population who was not and most nights his frustrated hoot could be heard from the trees outside.

A few days after her return, my mother noticed that Dee had difficulty in landing, especially onto the wrist, where she had trouble gripping tight. Her right leg was hot and swollen at the knee joint. Dr Garnet came immediately and decided that she had either broken or sprained it badly a few weeks before. He prescribed large and frequent doses of Abidec, much to the indignation of Dee who obviously hates this oily, health-sustaining medicine. By the time I returned from school she was her good old self once again.

Back at school, the news of Dee's return soon spread and from time to time a friend would ask how she was and what had made her return after so long. I could never answer this interesting question with any certainty. Had Dee come home because of her bad leg which prevented her catching food? So she had returned to be fed, or had she decided, with the approach of winter, that the nights would be warmer spent in our coach house rather than in a windswept cypress? Or had she felt some maternal call and come back to visit her home and have babies?

A few weeks later I left Eton for the last time. I packed my bags and left behind some of the happiest days of my life, cheered up only by the prospect of seeing Dee again.

I arrived home to be met by noisy squawks. What struck me at first sight was her change of colour and general bearing. She was no longer a deep reddy-brown but lighter with a definite chestnut tinge on the wing feathers. Her character also seemed to have changed and she strutted energetically about on my arm; a very different bird compared to the small, slightly nervous owl who had flown away seven months before. She was also far more friendly and seemed to show definite pleasure when I went to visit her, very often flying down to me even though it was not a mealtime.

BBC *Look East* telephoned to say they wanted Dee on their programme in three days and would I bring her to Norwich? Of course we said yes to the prospect of Dee becoming a screen personality, but I was worried at what might happen.

Dee was no longer the much-handled owl of a schoolboy's room of a year and a half ago. Then, she had been very much in public, on trains, in taxis and in stations. But now she was a highly strung, almost completely wild owl and I felt sure that a journey cooped up in a box in the car and being the subject of bright lights and strange moving machines would terrify her and perhaps make her desert us afterwards. Nevertheless, she was going on television and that was that. I just hoped that she would behave well and I cut her food down, thinking that an empty owl would be more manageable than a full one.

The evening before Dee's starring debut, our interviewer rang up to ask about her former life and to give me some idea as to how the following evening would be run. After a short conversation, he ended up by saying: 'Well, I'm glad you're bringing your owl, should give the viewers some idea what she was like.'

'Yes, I agree, but I am somewhat worried about her box as it might not fit in the car.'

'Why not take it out? It's not as if it's going to fly away, is it, being stuffed?'

'Being stuffed!' I replied in horror. 'You don't think she's stuffed, do you?'

'Well, what is she then? Alive?' he said in joking tones.

'Yes, very much so.'

'Oh, I see,' he said somewhat taken aback. 'Does she bite and scratch?' He sounded a trifle less confident.

'Sometimes,' I said.

'Oh . . . I see,' I heard him say after a short pause. 'Do you think it will behave tomorrow?'

'Frankly, no. But we can but hope and if she doesn't, well just too bad.'

'Oh dear,' he said nervously. 'I hope it does, as the studio is enormous and it might get caught up in all the wires on the ceiling.'

'I expect she'll behave,' I said encouragingly, feeling rather sorry for him, knowing quite well that not everybody has a passion for owls.

Next afternoon, much to her indignation and with squawks of complaint, we put Dee into the nest box I had made for her the year before and drove to Norwich. She behaved extremely well and her nerves compared with mine were calm, and she slept soundly until I put the box down in our changing room in the BBC's Norwich headquarters.

The atmosphere at *Look East* was a mixture of efficiency and casualness. All the people I met were outwardly carefree but, when on the job, worked like clockwork.

After a short wait, while we were charmingly entertained by a hostess, we were ushered into the studio. Dee was on my shoulder and apart from the occasional click at a strange object seemed surprisingly unmoved.

The studio was vast, not only in area but in height, and it was quite obvious that if Dee once left my shoulder it would be very difficult to extract her from the maze of arc lights, wires, and supporting rods. As I tightened my grip on the one jess I had put on her good foot to help control her, our interviewer introduced himself. He could not have been more helpful and put us at our ease. His meeting with Dee was not so congenial as Dee is not naturally polite.

An hour before the real appearance, there was the test run and we had our first taste of being in front of three cameras which drifted backwards and forwards on silent wheels; sometimes only four feet away from Dee's clicking beak. All went well until Dee, suddenly taking a violent dislike to an advancing camera, jumped off my arm only to be checked short by the jess which brought her squawking and flapping into my lap. I put her back on my wrist, from where she glared defiantly at the now retreating camera as if her display had frightened it away.

I stood up at the end of the test run in a cold sweat knowing quite well that Dee would have to behave much better during the real show. She was no longer calm but very much on the alert and somewhat nervous, looking at everything with an expression of horror. Once in the changing room again, I did my best to calm her and soon had her in her box where she retreated to the furthest corner. At that moment the door opened and a young girl announced that it was make-up time. 'Only for me I trust?' I queried, knowing perfectly well that it was, but Dee was worrying me at that moment.

The following three-quarters of an hour passed quickly and we were well entertained, but soon 'Everybody in the studio, please' came over the loudspeaker. Dee was extremely angry when I took her out of her box. She confirmed this, before I could put her jess back on by springing off my shoulder and swooping down a thirty-yard passage, causing several shouts and ducking heads and dropping a small wet hazard onto the floor on the way. She landed finally on my father's head, who fortunately happened to be waiting for me at the other end.

Two minutes later, we were all sitting in our allotted chairs waiting for the countdown with television cameras floating silently about in front of us. There were three groups in all: Dee and I first; a parish rector second who, as an expert on old musical instruments, was going to play some odd-looking contraption, and finally, a discussion between two men about some housing problem. Three minutes before zero-hour the stage manger told us to prepare ourselves. Two minutes was announced, then one minute. Meanwhile Dee was sitting very still on my right wrist, her claws biting deep. 30 seconds, 20 seconds, 10, 5, 4, 3, 2, Good luck everybody. Zero – and we were on.

I remember very little about the interview, what questions were asked and what I said, except that I was expecting Dee at any minute either to fly off in fright or to attack one of the cameras. Her talons gripped tighter and tighter around my wrist until I could feel her racing pulse through the thick skin of her foot. At last after some five minutes I heard the welcome words of our interviewer thanking us for coming and Dee's day of stardom was over.

But our troubles were far from over, as we had to sit absolutely still while the expert on old musical instruments performed some five yards away. As I began to whisper my congratulations to Dee, a very vulgar, lavatorial noise started only three yards from us, as the rector began to blow a black, snake-shaped instrument called a serpent. You can guess what it sounded like. This noise reduced our interviewer and me to fits of laughter, but for Dee it was the last straw and during the next five minutes she did her best to flee from this chamber of bright lights and terrifying noises. Mercilessly I fought with her because just two yards in front was a moving camera which had crept up on us without warning.

Half an hour later, an extremely exhausted Dee was on her way home to the comforting warmth of the coach house. The goodbyes of *Look East* had been said and remarks on Dee's good behaviour were frequent, but little did they know how easily she could have spoiled the whole show.

There was silence in the car speeding through the night, until quite suddenly Dee hooted; a small, soft, one-note hoot which could only have meant, 'Thank goodness that's over!' I thoroughly agreed with her.

Next morning Dee was not in the best of moods, refusing to eat anything. Rather concerned by this reaction to her television debut I left her alone for the day to recover. Her rest was short as I had completely forgotten that the *East Anglian Daily Times*, our local newspaper, had arranged to take photographs of her that day. More stardom for Dee, she was famous! So barely an hour later, accompanied by an enthusiastic photographer, I fetched a very disgruntled Dee from the coach house and took her down to our cellar as the best place for photography, for Dee's presence in the house had long been forbidden.

At first, Dee was far too sleepy to care what was happening and was quite happy sitting on my shoulder making a few gentle squeaks of protest. However, when the enthusiastic photographer produced his camera plus flashlight and then started jumping about making strange noises to attract her attention, Dee's attitude completely changed. She opened her eyes wide and with one look at the camera disappeared into one of the unlit passages of our cellar.

After a lengthy search, hindered by rakes and hoes, I eventually caught her in a dark passage. Gently placing her on my shoulder, I tried to turn her attention towards the photographer who, making vain efforts to look unconcerned, pressed the flash button causing once again the immediate flight of Dee into the darkness.

The result, after an hour, was several quickly taken photographs, two half-satisfied human beings and one very wild owl who I thought would never fly to me ever again. I put her into the coach house and left her shut in for several hours, hoping to give her time to forget her public life and become once more tame and friendly, which she so strangely had been since her return.

The next day I was in Marks and Spencer. The checkout girl smiled sweetly. 'You looked nice on telly last night.'

'Oh, thank you,' I said, flattered and blushing.

She smiled even more sweetly. 'But not as nice as your owl.'

What a downer that was!

For the next week I kept Dee in the harness room; first to let her recover and, now that she was home, because I wanted to be with her as much as possible. So I passed many an hour either talking to her or listening to her coo. She was so much stronger and her talons far sharper than before; my hands were soon covered with scratches. Every morning she greeted me with a long wavering hoot, having completely recovered in two days, and while I gave her a small breakfast of the usual liver and feathers, she would chatter away in a mixture of broken hoots, squawks and beak clicking. After this small meal she would sit, fluffing out her feathers, on my shoulder nibbling occasionally at my ear, which although hurting, I took for an affectionate caress. After more nibbles, she would fly up to her habitual perch, stand on one leg, blink a few times, yawn widely and go to sleep.

In the evening she was more active and after a meal of a mouse, a rat or some rabbit, would, in spite of a full stomach, walk and fly around the coach house inspecting corners and crannies that she had known all her life.

I was determined to keep her trained up and ready for when she would inevitably return to the wild. We invented a game, a sport really, that I called 'Hunt and Chase'. I'd catch a mouse alive and tie a short piece of string to its tail and then lie on my back on the floor of the harness room with Dee perched about fourteen feet above me. I would put the mouse beside me on the ground where it would hide between my back and the brick floor. Dee would be watching full of interest. At first Dee just stared fiercely, revolving her head. I then slowly pulled the mouse up onto my chest where it ran around in tight circles. This was too much for Dee and she launched herself in a thrilling swoop straight down. Thump! And what a whack to my chest it was. The mouse was dead instantly with the power of the pounce and the squeezing strength of Dee's talons. Then a fiddly tug o' war as I tried to untie the string from the mouse's tail while Dee tried to swallow it whole.

I felt rather sorry for the live mice but Dee's fitness was my priority. After a few triumphant kills by Dee, I reverted to laying dead ones on my chest to appease my conscience. Also the impact of Dee's pounce was surprisingly painful.

I couldn't resist taking my camera with me and,

pointing it upwards, tried to catch Dee as she swooped down. The photograph captioned 'Mouse in sight' is the result of many attempts.

My affection for Dee at this moment was the greatest it had ever been.

At the end of this week of captivity, the longest since she had left Eton, I opened the harness-room door satisfied that her leg was strong enough for her to go out. Once again she was in the wild, where she was born. Her only difference from other owls was that she could come and go between her life in the wild and that in the coach house.

Few people, as I have already said, realise what owls get up to. An experiment carried out in England discovered that the owls in the region surveyed destroy annually 9,260 rodents in just under one square mile. I repeat: nine thousand two hundred and sixty, the population of a large village. Also, the result of another specialist's experiment might interest some of the many cat lovers in the country. As to the destruction of rodents, one owl is worth a good twelve of their sacred, fireside-warmed-up mogs.

I am not suggesting that people should discard their cats and take owls instead as pets. No, please not! It is just a gentle plea that gamekeepers, keen young shots or bloodthirsty youths with air guns should resist the temptation to slaughter a slow-flying owl carrying out its natural role in the balance of nature. Gamekeepers are the more guilty as the owl's sharp talons immediately make them imagine that all birds with claws and curved beaks are out to kill their sacred charges. They don't realise that owls do not begin hunting till it's almost dark, when baby pheasants and partridges are safely under their mother's wing. Surely rats destroy more game chicks than any other predator. *And* rats, by the way, happen to be owl food

With some apprehension, I walked to the coach house the morning after I had opened the door to the outside world and was so pleased to be greeted with the usual hoot. She flew down but, not being hungry, refused the food I offered and returned to her perch.

Dee has changed. No longer is she excessively friendly; she's shy and rather aloof; much the same as before her departure seven months ago. Does this mean that she is about to go away again and not make a nest in the coach house as we've all so hoped? I did not shut her up but instead began to give her an enormous meal at night in an effort to keep her from her nightly wanderings, which were, without doubt, encouraged by another member of the garden's owl population. This particular one could be heard at about five o'clock every evening, hooting from an oak tree right beside the coach house.

He was by no means the first, the next two months witnessing a series of feathered suitors waiting for their 'date'. Dee seemed to play hard to get, and took advantage of hiding within our protection. Our efforts to attract her consisted of offering delicious morsels of food, such as shot pigeon, a run-over duck and suchlike, all of which she devoured energetically. She'd make a pigeon last for as much as three days.

A week after her release, I had to leave for a long stay in France. As usual my farewell to Dee was painful, although I knew my mother would take faithful care and send regular news. And I was pleased that, after all the difficulties, we had succeeded in returning both the owls to the wild able to look after themselves. With their hearing, their eyesight and their silent flight, they are quite different from other birds of prey, and they are masters of the night.

Some weeks later, in Aix-en-Provence, I received the exciting news that Dee was singing her love song and frequenting the nesting box. How wonderful. I inwardly congratulated the successful suitor who had captured her charms. Not only would we have some more charming owlets, but it would be a triumph to have owls breeding so close by. Unfortunately, either owing to the infidelity of the suitor or her own incapacity, Dee didn't produce any eggs and the nesting box could only boast of a small chicken's egg put there as encouragement and one or two rat skulls left over from last year.

After a week or two of cooing from her box, Dee returned to the life she had led a year ago, when I wrote the earlier chapters; coming and going in and out of the wild. She is much the same owl as then, except stronger and more beautiful. She is in the coach house two days out of three. Strangely enough these absences don't affect her friendliness and as the anniversary of her entry into my life has just passed for the second time, I am once again wondering where fortune will have taken her by this time next year.

Anyhow she will be back tomorrow.

MAY 1961

Epilogue

MANY, MANY YEARS later, after my return from South America, yet again an unknown donor dumped three baby owls on our doorstep in the usual unlabelled cardboard box. We gave them names from opera and they became very tame indeed, and my children adored them. When they were old enough to fly, a violent thunderstorm blew one of them away – we never found him. The two survivors would fly to my shoulder at the whistle. One late summer evening, an old friend came to supper; we were eating with all the windows open. I asked him if he believed in ghosts. 'Of course not,' he said. I stretched out my arm and whistled. Out of the dark and in through the open window without a sound flew Siegmund and Sieglinde and landed – *thump, thump* – side by side on my arm. My friend's cheeks paled.